The Argument Builder

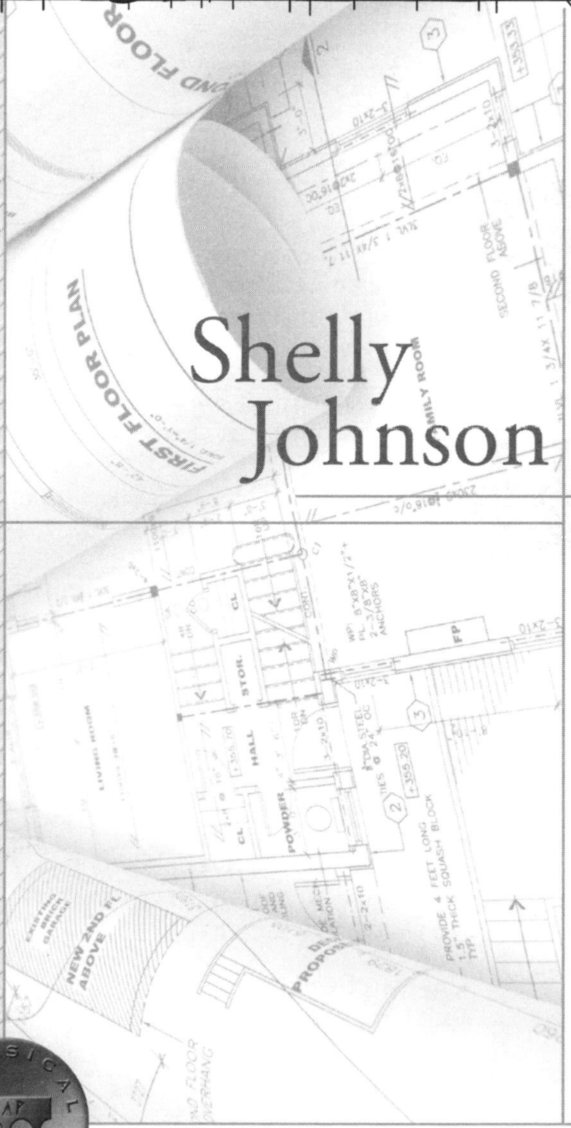

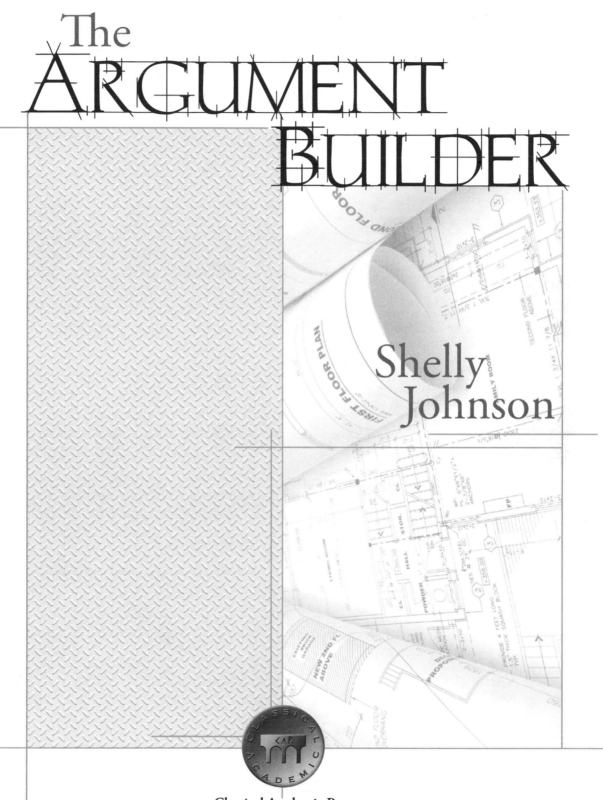

Shelly Johnson

Classical Academic Press
Camp Hill, Pennsylvania

www.ClassicalAcademicPress.com

The Argument Builder

Version 1.0

ISBN: 1-60051-026-4
EAN: 9781600510267

Cover art by Rob Baddorf
Interior design by Lenora Riley

Classical Academic Press
2151 Market Street
Camp Hill, PA 17011

www.ClassicalAcademicPress.com

I would like to dedicate this book to
My husband, John Johnson
My parents, Bill and Faye Pruitt and John and Diane Johnson
and Trinity Christian Academy

The publisher wishes to extend its gratitude to
Lauraine Gustafson, who edited this text

Table of Contents

FOREWORD

All of us need to make good arguments now and then. Few of us, however, have been trained in the art of building a strong and persuasive argument. Even those people who seem naturally "good at arguing" could benefit from some excellent training. That is what *The Argument Builder* seeks to do: train you in the art of building a strong argument.

When a house is built, the workers consult a step-by-step plan. Materials are assembled and arranged, equipment is brought to the building site, then a hole is dug for the laying of the foundation of the structure. First the foundation, then the frame, then the roof, then the plumbing and electrical lines are installed. Next, the walls are completed, insulated and covered, and the windows are installed. Finally, the finishing work is completed inside the house, which involves fine carpentry and installing fixtures and appliances.

Crafting a good argument may not be as detailed or time-consuming as building a house, but it does involve planning, gathering materials, and assembling the whole in an orderly, compelling manner. Once you become skilled at argument building, you will find yourself building strong arguments quickly and efficiently.

In this book, you will be shown how to plan and build good arguments. You will study excellent examples of some very good argument makers indeed—talented people ranging from classical Greek and Roman orators to biblical writers, Shakespeare, Bacon, Montaigne, and contemporary writers. You will learn what materials to use: examples, statistics, experts, proverbs, analogies, difference, degree, and cause and effect, among others. Using these materials, you will have ample opportunity to practice building good arguments both by studying the masters and seeking to imitate them in your own arguments. You will even have a chance to engage in a debate with your fellow students when you finish the book.

While *The Argument Builder* specializes in building good arguments, its companion text, *The Art of Argument*, specializes in detecting what is wrong in bad arguments. *The Argument Builder* will review some of the fallacies studied in *The Art of Argument*, but you may want to work through *The Art of Argument* to round out your study of arguments. You may also want to study *The Discovery of Deduction*, our formal logic text that examines the correct form logical arguments should take. To see samples of these books please visit the website of Classical Academic Press at www.classicalacademicpress.com.

Enjoy your study of *The Argument Builder*. Soon you will be well prepared for building, supporting, and presenting a well-formed argument.

Christopher A. Perrin, Ph.D.
Publisher

INTRODUCTION *to Students*

Have you ever wanted to prove a point but you didn't know how to do it? Have you ever been stuck in an argument in which your opponent seems to have all the valid points but you don't know what to say? If so, this is just the book for you.

This book will teach you an argument-discovery method called **common topics**, which was created by **Aristotle**, one of the greatest thinkers of all time. The common topics present for exploration a list of categories or "lines of argument" that allow you to discover all the possible arguments for your topic.

To help you understand how we will proceed, let me give you an idea of the pattern of this book. Each unit will introduce one of the common topics. Every topic has several subtopics that demonstrate more clearly how the topic can be used. In addition, for many of the common topics, you will also learn some common **fallacies**, or errors in reasoning, committed with these topics. By studying these fallacies, you will learn to form strong arguments from the common topics without falling into some common traps of bad reasoning.

In each chapter, you will read about how you can use a particular common topic and its subtopics to develop a hypothetical argument about curfew (a rule that governs what time you must be in your house at night). As you move through the book, each chapter will use the curfew example to help you understand how the common topic works practically. At the end of each chapter, you will find other examples of the topic, and you will practice using them to develop arguments. After you have completed this book, you will be well on your way to mastering an argument-building method that will be an excellent tool for you to use for the rest of your life.

Imagine this scenario: You have just passed your driver's test, and you are now the proud owner of a license. You are excited about your new freedom and can't wait to go out on the weekends to drive around and hang out with your friends. You are certain that you are entering one of the most thrilling times in your life. Then, you hear the bad news: your parents are a little nervous about your driving alone, and they have set your weekend curfew at 10:00 p.m.—the same time your curfew was even before you got your driver's license. You are crushed! After all, you are nearly an adult, so it seems like you should get a few more privileges. A 12:00 a.m. weekend curfew seems much more reasonable to you. After all, all of your other driving friends have midnight curfews. However, you know, instinctively, not to try that line of argument. Whenever you do try the "But all my other friends…" argument, your mother always responds in the same basic way, with some creative variations: "If all your friends jumped off a bridge, robbed a bank, sold themselves into slavery, pierced their big toe would you do it, too?"

Right now, you may be contemplating two equally unappealing options: committing yourself to a life of mopey martyrdom or throwing the grandest, most spectacular tantrum of your life. Neither of these courses is recommended. Instead, you might consider a third option of presenting a civil, well-reasoned argument for a 12:00 a.m. curfew. After all, the worst that your parents can say is "no," and they may actually be interested in hearing your opinion, especially if your standard M.O. (from the Latin *modus operandi* meaning "standard way of operating") is to try the mopey martyrdom or tantrum options. How would you construct this hypothetical, well-reasoned argument? After all, your best argument up to now has been the "But all my friends are doing it" argument, and that is getting you nowhere. Where would you find good points to which your parents would actually listen? How would you know which arguments were your best ones? How would you know how to state them properly?

In order to find the answers to these questions, it may help if you learn a little more about the famous philosopher, Aristotle, and two of his favorite topics: **logic** and **rhetoric**. Aristotle lived in Athens, Greece, in 384-322 BC.[1] In Aristotle's day, people were becoming more and more fascinated with **rhetoric**, which is the art of effective public speaking. As people joined the profession of rhetoric, they developed different concepts of what defined good rhetoric. For instance, the **sophists** were one group of **rhetoricians**, or public speakers, who focused more on the sound and style of their speeches, rather than on the content.[2] While there is nothing wrong, per se (in itself), with this approach, many other rhetoricians considered the sophists' arguments shallow. In fact, even today, if someone says that an argument is "sophistic," he means that the argument is shallow.

Aristotle did not agree with the sophists' approach to rhetoric, and was instead extremely concerned with the *content* of speeches. He wanted to help his students find all of the available arguments for a given topic. In order to do this, he wrote about something called the common topics, a set of argument categories that a person can use to discover evidence for an argument. The main categories of common topics are: **definitions**, **testimony**, **comparison**, **relationship**, and **circumstance**.[3] Each of these main categories contains several subtopics. For example, under the common topic of comparison, Aristotle discussed **analogy**, **difference**, and **degree**. Aristotle believed that **logicians** and rhetoricians could use these topics to help them create the best arguments possible.

However, awareness of the common topics was not enough. Good rhetoricians also had to be able to reason well using the common topics, so Aristotle also taught about logic in order to help his students use the common topics properly. Logic can be defined as "the art and science of reasoning."[4] In his book *Rhetoric*, Aristotle described two types of logic that people can use to develop the common topics properly.[5] Today we call these two types of logic **deductive** and **inductive**.

BUT I ALREADY KNOW HOW TO WIN AN ARGUMENT... I JUST YELL REALLY LOUD.
Logic 101

Deductive logic comes from the Latin word *deducere*, which means "to draw down." In other words, deductive arguments "draw down" knowledge contained by, or inherent in, a previously stated fact. To help you understand deductive logic better, let's look at the main tool used with this kind of logic: the **syllogism**. A syllogism is an argument that contains a **conclusion**, which is a statement of belief, supported by two **premises**, which are facts used as evidence. The following is a common example of a syllogism:

All men are mortal.

Socrates is a man.

Therefore, Socrates is mortal.

The basic idea of deductive logic is that if the first two statements are true then the last statement must also be true. It is a logical conclusion that follows from the first two statements. That is, the first two statements imply, or point to, the last statement. We could also say that the conclusion is inherent in, or an essential characteristic of, the premises. Deductive logic is a very precise type of logic. If the premises are true, and the argument is arranged properly, then the conclusion must be true.

The second type of logic—inductive logic—is what will be emphasized in this book. The word "inductive" comes from the Latin word *inducere*, which means "to lead to." Inductive arguments are the opposite of deductive arguments. Rather than drawing down knowledge already implied in facts or statements, inductive logic leads us to generalize on observations or examples that we see in everyday circumstances. In other words, inductive logic helps us recognize general patterns and theories that everyday observations or examples indicate.

Many medical and nutritional studies are based on inductive logic. For instance, you have certainly heard people quoting studies that indicate that smoking cigarettes is linked with a high chance of developing lung cancer.

In order to make this conclusion, researchers surveyed hundreds and thousands of people who smoked, and they noticed that a high percentage of them ended up with lung cancer. Of course, these same researchers did additional research to make sure that no other factors, such as pollution or diet, were causing the lung cancer. Once they eliminated other possible sources, and determined smoking as a common habit of all the lung cancer victims, they could establish fairly conclusively that smoking caused the lung cancer. If you refer back to the definition of "inductive logic," you can see that it is the basis of the researchers' conclusion because they observed many examples of lung cancer patients who smoked, and those observations indicated a pattern of smoking as a cause for lung cancer. Just as syllogisms are the foundation of deductive logic, examples are the foundation of inductive logic.

You may notice that inductive arguments are not as precise as deductive arguments. No matter how many convincing examples you observe, there still may be some other example that disproves your point. However, if you learn to structure your inductive arguments well, your arguments will be extremely strong, even if they are not 100 percent certain. Our examination of the common topics and their subtopics will help you understand how to use them to construct strong and effective arguments.

Right now, you might feel a little uncomfortable with the word **argument** because it seems that it always involves fighting, tension, hostility, and hurt feelings. Although this unpleasantness can be present when people argue, it doesn't have to be. The Latin word *argumentum* simply means "evidence" or "proof." Therefore, when you have an "argument," it means that you supply the evidence or proof for what you believe. When people state their conclusions and premises clearly and logically, it can actually help prevent tension and hostility. In fact, as you will see in the next chapter, it is important to approach debates and arguments with an attitude of humility and self-awareness. One of the most important things you can realize before you debate is that you might be wrong, and your opponent might be right.

Before we move on, it is important for you to realize that good logic requires two key skills. The first skill is building good arguments, which is the focus of this book. The second skill is detecting whether or not the other person's argument is a good argument or if it contains fallacies, which are "commonly recognized types of bad arguments."[6] When someone commits a fallacy, his premise does not lead to his conclusion. In this book, we will examine some of the most common fallacies connected with each of the common topics. If you haven't already, I would recommend that you also study *The Art of Argument*, which is a companion text to this book. In that book, you will learn dozens of fallacies that people often commit. Learning those fallacies will not only help you sharpen your argument skills, it will also help you to avoid them in your own arguments. When you learn to build good arguments and to critique others' arguments, you will be well prepared to engage in and analyze the arguments you hear every day.

Deductive logic comes from the Latin word deducere, *which means "to draw down."*

DEFINE

1. Logic: ______________________________

2. Rhetoric: ______________________________

3. Sophists: ______________________________

4. Common Topics: ______________________________

RESEARCH

Research these other famous Greek and Roman rhetoricians and summarize their views and their contributions to rhetoric.

1. Demosthenes: ______________________________

2. Protagoras: ______________________________

3. Gorgias: ______________________________

4. Isocrates: ______________________________

5. Quintilian: ______________________________

6. Cicero: ______________________________

CONSIDER

Rhetoric surrounds you every day in speeches, commercials, advertisements, and writing. Considering what you know about the rhetoric of today, do you think it is more in line with sophistic (focus on style) or Aristotelian (focus on content) views on rhetoric? Give two examples to support your idea.

DESCRIBE

Describe two strengths and two weaknesses of both sophistic and Aristotelian ideas of rhetoric.

At this point, you may believe that the main reason to learn logic is so that you can win arguments. That is a common misconception. The most important reason for you to learn logic is to help you understand what is right and true. This is an important distinction to understand. If your main goal in argumentation is to win, you may, inadvertently, commit fallacies and miss the point.

To help you understand this better, there is something important that you should know about yourself: you are very easily deceived, especially by yourself. Don't worry, it's not just you—all human beings are easily deceived. In fact, a man named **Francis Bacon**, who lived from 1561 to 1626, believed that human beings tend to deceive themselves and that they must continually work to free themselves from flawed thinking.[1] He was one of the earliest proponents, or supporters, of the scientific method (yes, you have him to thank for all of those science fair projects and experiments you have done), and he was interested in how people think and search for truth. He developed the scientific method to help people overcome their flawed thinking. In order to help people understand the ways they deceive themselves, Bacon wrote about something that he called the **four idols**.[2]

An idol is something that people worship. Webster's dictionary defines an **idol** as "a false god; a false conception; an object of extreme devotion." In ancient cultures, and in some cultures today, many people worshipped idols made of stone, gold, or other precious metals. When Francis Bacon wrote about the four idols, however, he was not referring to golden or stone images. Instead, he was describing ideas or habits we hold dear that can hinder our ability to think clearly. In other words, our devotion to these ideas and habits can cause us to be prejudiced or biased.[3] Webster's dictionary defines a **prejudice** as a "preconceived judgment or opinion," and a **bias** as a "highly personal and unreasoned distortion of judgment." The four idols Bacon described were the **idols of the tribe**, the **idols of the cave**, the **idols of the marketplace**, and the **idols of the theatre**.[4] As you read about these idols, you may be surprised at how they affect your life and thinking.

The first group of idols, known as the idols of the tribe, is made up of the faults that are common to all human beings. You might think of a tribe as a group of people who live in a certain part of the world. Bacon used the term "tribe" to refer to the whole human race. In other words, Bacon believed that the idols of the tribe were weaknesses that every single human being has in common. These are weaknesses such as **wishful thinking** and **hasty generalization**. For instance, Bacon wrote that our senses are weak and easily deceived, and he said that humans tend to engage in wishful thinking. By this, he meant that we have a natural tendency to accept what we would like to be true or what we believe is true.[5] For instance, did you know that researchers recently have claimed that chocolate, especially dark chocolate, can be good for your health?[6] You might find yourself eager to believe this study because you like chocolate and, if the study is true, you could eat chocolate three meals a day. However, just because you want something to be true doesn't mean it is true. This example illustrates a general tendency of human beings: we like to believe things that are pleasant and comfortable to us, and we don't want to believe things that are unpleasant or uncomfortable to us. In this case, our idol, or our object of extreme devotion, is our physical or emotional comfort. We care about our comfort and pleasure so much that it can prevent us from seeing unpleasant or uncomfortable truths.

The second group of idols is the idols of the cave. These are faulty thinking patterns that come from our specific backgrounds and social groups. Bacon called these the "idols of the cave" because our upbringing is like a cave that can limit our perceptions of the rest of the world. For example, each of us has been raised in a particular social class (lower, middle, or upper), and we all belong to a certain ethnic group (Caucasian, Asian, African American, Hispanic, Native American, etc., or a mixture of these groups). Whatever our background, we have learned to believe certain things about ourselves, the world, other people, and other groups based on the beliefs and practices of our specific group. Because of this, it is often hard for us to understand the viewpoints of other groups.[7]

For example, poor people often have misconceptions about rich people. They might believe that all rich people are spoiled or have been given their wealth by relatives. They also might believe that all wealthy people are happy. In reality, however, many wealthy people become wealthy by working hard in demanding jobs. Also, not all wealthy people are happy. There are plenty of miserable wealthy people. Many wealthy people also have misconceptions about poor people, such as that all poor people are poor because they are lazy. They might also think that poor people are unhappy because they don't have a lot of money. In reality, many poor people are extremely hard workers who work several jobs just to make ends meet. Also, many poor people are happy because they have great friends and families, and they love their jobs, even though they don't pay very well.

As another example, consider that people who have been raised in Republican families may not understand why people would be Democrats, while people raised in Democratic families may not understand why anyone would vote Republican. These two groups may not understand each other, yet there are intelligent and moral people in both. These examples demonstrate that it can be difficult for us to understand people who hold viewpoints that are different than our own. The idols of the cave represent the cave of our own opinion, which can blind us to the truth in other viewpoints.

The third group of idols, the idols of the marketplace, represents the way in which words can be deceiving. For example, let's say that you decide to go to a popular new movie with a friend. Because tickets for the movie will sell quickly, you tell your friend to get to the movie early so that you can get good seats. In your mind, "early" means "at least fifteen minutes early and maybe twenty," but your friend is a bit of a procrastinator. When she arrives a mere five minutes early, you are upset with her. Your friend cannot understand why you are annoyed; after all, she did get there early. As you can see, sometimes words like "early" can be imprecise because they mean different things to different people. Bacon realized that in order to think clearly, people must clearly define words and use them precisely.[8] However, Bacon also realized that translating our thoughts effectively into words so that others can understand us can be more difficult than it seems.

Sometimes we use words that have several different definitions, such as in the case above. Sometimes we use words that mean something to us but that are unfamiliar to other people. He called word errors like this the "idols of the marketplace." This may seem like an odd title for these errors, but if you think of a marketplace, or a place where people buy and sell things, it may help you understand why he named this kind of error the way he did. When someone tries to sell an object or a service to someone, the salesman must carefully communicate the benefits and value of what he is selling. If he uses words that his customer doesn't understand or words that can mean more than one thing, he will confuse and possibly even lose his customer.

A similar thing happens when we discuss ideas with other people. We aren't *selling* ideas to them, but we are trying to get them to accept, or at least understand, our opinion. People will not be able to do this if we speak over their heads or use words with many possible meanings. That is why it is so important that we use words carefully.

The last set of idols Bacon wrote about were the idols of the theatre. These idols represent "the human tendency to prefer older, more widely accepted ideas over novel, minority opinions."[9] Bacon believed that people often develop whole philosophies based on a few observations, rather than doing a thorough, scientific investigation. Bacon also believed that once people develop a philosophy or a **paradigm**—a model for understanding part of life, nature, or the universe—it is difficult for them to see past this philosophy, and it can blind them to the truth.[10] An example of this would be the geocentric, or earth-centered, theory of the universe, which most people believed until the 1500s. Ancient philosophers observed the earth, planets, and stars and determined that the earth was the center of the universe. This was a fairly reasonable conclusion given the instruments and abilities they had to investigate these matters at the time. However, this model of thinking became so fixed in peoples' minds that when scientists, such as Copernicus and Galileo, demonstrated that the sun was the center of the universe, it was difficult for people to give up their belief in the old model. Many people still believed that the earth was the center of the universe and even refused to look at evidence that contradicted that theory.[11]

We often look at examples like this and believe that we could not be similarly deceived. However, instances such as these still occur. For example, even as late as the mid-1800s, people did not understand the link between germs and disease. During the Civil War, it was common for doctors to operate on several different patients without washing their hands between surgeries. Of course, this contributed to a high rate of infection and death among their patients. Because doctors at that time did not fully understand the connection between germs and disease, it was very hard for them to accept this connection, even when people like Florence Nightingale (a Civil War-era nurse famous for championing the adoption of improved medical hygiene) presented good evidence for better hygiene. As these examples demonstrate, the idols of the theatre represent our love for our personal philosophies.[12]

These four idols point to the need we all have to gain wisdom.

As you can imagine, every single one of us is affected by these idols at some time in our life. As we become more aware of ways in which our thinking can be clouded and deceived, it helps us think more clearly. It is important for you to know that you are especially easy to deceive when you are very passionate or emotional about a topic. There is nothing wrong with emotions, per se, but when we are emotional about a particular topic and desperately want to prove a certain point, it is easy for us to use fallacies, especially if they seem to help us prove our point. As we carefully examine in later chapters each of the fallacies that are connected with the common topics, it will help you to avoid deceiving yourself.

The four idols and their effects on our way of thinking point to the need we all have to gain wisdom. If logic is a tool every person can use, then we can use the tool either wisely or foolishly. Too often, people misuse logic to manipulate, deceive, and attack other people. Logic can be a dangerous weapon or a wonderful tool. I hope that as you proceed through the rest of this book, you will resist the temptation of these four idols and fine-tune your ability to properly use the extraordinary tool that is logic.

As we wrap up this chapter, let's quickly relate the idols to the curfew debate we have been considering. At this point, you feel that your parents' proposed curfew is unfair and that they should be a little bit more lenient with you now that you are older. It is possible that you are right about this. After all, parents are human, and sometimes they make rules that are less than ideal or that are overprotective. However, it is important that you realize that you may be wrong, too. You also are human, and you might think that you are ready for more responsibility than you really are. Also, if you are honest with yourself, you will realize that your parents probably know much more about the potential dangers of driving at night than you do.

If you examine your thoughts and emotions, you may realize that it is difficult to see past your strong opinions and beliefs or to even think about your parents' point of view. If you can see this, you will understand that you are being affected by the idols that Francis Bacon described. If you approach the curfew debate determined to win and prove your parents wrong, you are already starting down the wrong path. Instead, you need to approach the curfew debate with the goal of using logic to state your point well, understand your parents' reasoning, and reach a good conclusion together.

ANSWER

Who was Francis Bacon? ______________________________

EXPLAIN

In your own words, explain each of the four idols and how they can distort our thinking.

1. Idols of the Tribe: ______________________________

2. Idols of the Cave: ______________________________

3. Idols of the Marketplace: ______________________________

4. Idols of the Theatre: ______________________________

DEFINE

1. Bias: ______________________________

2. Prejudice: ______________________________

DESCRIBE

Think of a time when you were affected by one of the four idols. You may have noticed the idols clouding your judgment, or you may have noticed them clouding the judgment of someone else. Describe what happened, how it affected you personally, and then write down which idol affected the situation.

LIST

List three or four words people often use that can be easily defined in several different ways. Explain how these different meanings could result in conflict.

Common Topic 1

Definitions

If you are a person who loves to argue and debate, you might immediately assemble all of your arguments and fire them off at your opponent as though you were executing a military drill. If so, you are missing the most important step in any debate: definition. When you are getting ready to argue there are two important things that you must define: your position and the key terms in your position. Because this step is so important, definition is the first common topic we will examine. It is not exactly a type of argument, but it is an important preparatory step you need to take as you begin to argue.

The following are concepts that will be helpful to understand as you read the next chapter.

Thesis statement: A declarative statement of opinion that can be proven true or false.

Definition: An explanation or illustration of a word. There are several ways to define a word: **genus**, **species**, **etymology**, **synonyms**, **antonyms**, **description**, and **examples**.

You may not believe me right now, but once you learn how to define terms properly and clearly state your thesis, you will save yourself and anyone with whom you debate a world of frustration.

CHAPTER 3 *Definitions*

When did your mom and dad last ask you to clean your room? When you finished cleaning, were they pleased with the result? If you are like many teenagers, you have discovered that your definition of the word "clean" varies greatly from your parents' definition of it. You may typically define "clean" as "to shove all the dirty clothes to one corner and all books, plates, and other unidentifiable objects under your bed and in the closet." Your parents, on the other hand, seem to define clean as "to make sure your bed is made and all surfaces are spotless and junk-free." As you have most likely discovered, this difference in definitions can cause miscommunication, which can lead to problems. Believe it or not, differing definitions not only cause small-scale interpersonal problems like the ones you may have with your parents over the condition of your room, but they have, throughout history, even caused wars.

Defining the terms of your argument will not solve all of your conflicts, but it can prevent a lot of confusion. In order to define your topic carefully, there are three main steps you need to take. First, you must determine what it is you believe about your topic. This is your conclusion. Second, you will write a declarative statement about your conclusion that can be proven true or false. This is your thesis statement. By "declarative statement" I mean a sentence that is a statement of fact rather than a question or a command. Third, once you have your thesis statement developed, you should then define the key terms within the position you have stated.

Every argument or debate that you ever have should proceed from a thesis statement. Here are some examples:

- Teenagers with driver's licenses should have a 12:00 a.m. weekend curfew.
- Teenagers with driver's licenses should have a 10:00 p.m. weekend curfew.
- Requiring students to wear school uniforms establishes a disciplined atmosphere.
- Requiring students to wear school uniforms inhibits students' creativity and freedom of expression.
- Capital punishment is a biblical mandate.
- Capital punishment is not a biblical mandate.

As you can see, these statements all make a claim that is possible to prove true or false. In order to have a successful argument, it is crucial that you have a clear thesis statement. As odd as it may seem, it is possible for people to begin an argument believing they are discussing the same topic only to discover later on that they are actually discussing two different ideas. This can cause a lot of confusion and wasted time. By developing a clear thesis statement before you begin your argument, you can avoid this potential problem.

In some debates, you may be able to state your thesis statement before you do any further research. However, sometimes it is necessary to define the key terms of your debate before you can form your thesis statement. Before you attempt to form your thesis statement for your curfew debate, let's look at some techniques you can use to define words thoroughly and properly. It is important to define key terms for all topics because people often have different definitions for common terms. For instance, people have widely varying definitions of seemingly straightforward terms, such as "patriotism," "love," "discipline," "art," "music," "freedom," "Christianity" and "school." Once you define clearly what you mean by a word, it will be much easier to discuss it productively. For example, if you want to make a new proposal to your parents about curfew, it is essential to define exactly what they mean by "curfew." Do they mean that you must be in bed by 10:00 p.m. or just home by that time? Do they mean that you must be in your house, or could you be in a friend's house? Their definition of "curfew" will certainly determine the arguments you will use.

When you define your key term or terms, it is extremely important that you form a good, basic definition that allows you to proceed with the argument. Often, the best place to find this type of definition is in a good dictionary. For instance, Webster's *Ninth New Collegiate Dictionary* defines "curfew" as "the time that the curfew signal is sounded; a signal (usually a bell) announcing the start of curfew restrictions; or an order that after a specific time certain activities (as those being outside on the streets) are prohibited." For your debate with your parents, you will be discussing the third definition of "curfew": "an order that after a specific time certain activities (as those being outside on the streets) are prohibited."

After further inquiry, you realize that your parents want you to be in your house by 10:00 p.m., although you don't have to be in your bed at that time. You may also, at times, be in other people's houses at curfew time if you have received permission ahead of time from your parents to stay the night at someone else's house. Therefore, your working definition of "curfew" with your parents is: "A rule that requires you to be in your house, or a previously approved house, by 10:00 p.m."

If your argument is short, as your debate with your parents most likely will be, a dictionary definition may be an adequate enough definition for you to proceed with the argument. However, if you are engaging in a long argument, such as when you participate in a lengthy debate or write a long thesis paper, you may need to use other definition techniques. In these cases, it can be extremely helpful for you to ask and answer the following questions about the word or words that will be essential to your topic:

- Where did this word come from?
- What has been its common meaning throughout history?
- What kind of group does this thing belong to?
- What other words or concepts are like it?
- What are other words or concepts that are unlike it?
- How do you do it?
- What are some everyday illustrations of this concept?
- What does it look like?

Some of the most common definition techniques you can use to answer these questions are genus, species, etymology, synonyms, antonyms, descriptions, and examples. As I mentioned before, it is unlikely that you will use all of these techniques in your short discussion with your parents on curfew, but for the sake of illustration, we will examine them so that you can use them in other arguments.

One of the most helpful definition techniques is that of genus and species. The "genus" of a word is the larger group to which it belongs. For instance, lions, tigers, and Siamese cats, all belong to the genus of "cat." Blue, yellow, and green belong to the genus of "color." Mansions, cottages, and townhouses belong to the genus of "homes." When we refer to "species," we discuss the characteristics of a word that make it different from the other species in its genus. For instance, if we were discussing the different species in the genus of "cat," we might discuss differentiating characteristics, such as size, predatory habits, and habitats. If we were to discuss different species in the genus of "house," we might discuss square footage and architectural characteristics.

If we look at our argument about curfew, we could say that the term "curfew" is under the genus of "rules." It is like other rules, such as dress code, socializing rules, and entertainment rules. A curfew differs specifically, however, because it is a rule that governs when you come and go from your house at night. Furthermore, curfew rules usually affect teenagers or young adults, rather than children or adults. Discussing the genus and species of a term can help you to pinpoint the most important elements of your topic. This can be especially helpful when a term is unfamiliar to the person with whom you are debating.

Another definition technique is etymology, which is the history and origin of a word. To better understand what etymology is, it may be helpful to know that many of our English words came from other languages, such as Greek, Latin, or French. That is, we have many derivatives, or words that come from other languages, in our English language. Take the word "derivative," for instance. It is actually a derivative itself. It comes from two Latin words *de*, which means "down from" and *rivus*, which means "river." So, the word "derivative" literally means "down from the river." Knowing the background of this word helps us to better understand its definition, and paints us a picture of the Latin and French languages as great rushing rivers full of words, some of which have flown into other language rivers, such as English. Using etymology when building an argument can be helpful because it can aid you in understanding what a word means. Pastors often share the etymology of certain words in their sermons in order to help their congregations understand a particular passage, as do teachers when they are seeking to clarify a concept. Keep in mind that etymology is not always useful or helpful in an argument or debate. For instance, when you are debating something in everyday life, or a similarly informal setting, it may be odd to share the etymology of a word. However, if you are participating in a formal debate or writing a formal paper, it is proper to be more academic, and discussing etymology can be helpful.

If you are participating in a formal debate or writing a formal paper, it is proper to be more academic, and discussing etymology can be helpful.

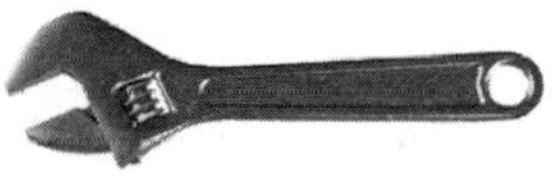

For the sake of example, let's look at the etymology of the word "curfew." It comes from the Old French word *cuevrefeu* or *covrir*, which means "to cover." It can also mean "to cover the fire" (*feu* is "fire" in French). This helps us better understand why a curfew is a rule that requires someone to be at home because, based on its word of origin, it means that it is time, literally, "to cover the fire," an action people used to do as they prepared for going to bed.

Description is another useful definition device. When people use description, they explain a word in greater detail than what is available in the word's definition. To better illustrate the term "curfew," you could describe some of the different types of curfews parents have set for their children. For example, you know that some parents allow their teenagers, especially older ones, to come home at all

JUST REMEMBER,
IF ANYONE ASKS, IT'S NOT
A SLUMBER PARTY, IT'S A
"SOCIAL EXPERIMENT."

hours of the night. Other parents, especially those whose families live in a dangerous part of town, may require their children to be in by dark in order to avoid the dangerous activities that can occur after nightfall. A majority of other parents require their teens to be at home or in a previously approved house by midnight and to call their parents when they reach the pre-approved location. Some parents allow their teenagers to be out as late as 2 a.m. on a weekend, but only if they are coming back from a previously approved activity, such as watching a movie with friends. Description can be a useful definition technique because it shows the range of possibilities for a given topic. Examining these possibilities can help people to make better decisions.

A definition technique closely related to description is example. When you give an example of your topic, you focus on one instance that clearly illustrates the word you are trying to define. This is different from description because description focuses on many different instances, while an example focuses specifically on one instance to illustrate a word. If you were giving an example of curfew, you might say, "My friend, David, has an interesting weekend curfew arrangement with his parents. When he first got his driver's license, he was required to be in his house or a previously approved friend's house by 11:00 p.m. If he was away from home, his parents also required him to call to let them know he was at the approved house. However, as he demonstrated responsibility, he earned greater curfew privileges. Therefore, after following his initial curfew responsibly for three months, David earned an extended curfew. After following this rule responsibly for the next three months, he was no longer required to check in with his parents. He continued to renegotiate with his parents every few months, and after a year or so, he earned the privilege to be out until 2:00 a.m. on the weekends as long as his grades did not suffer during the week." Providing an in-depth example like this can be very helpful and can aid further discussion.

Genus, species, etymology, description, and example are some of the most common definition techniques that you can use to explain your topic. Other helpful definition techniques include synonyms, antonyms, and procedural or operational definitions.

Synonyms are words that have the same or similar meanings as other words. As we noted earlier in this chapter, there are some words, such as the word "love," which can have different meanings to different people. Using a synonym for the word "love," such as "affection" or "devotion," can help others understand how you are using the word "love" in a discussion or argument.

Antonyms, which are words that have the opposite meaning of another word, can also be used to clarify the meaning of a word you are using. For instance, by pointing out that an antonym of the word "love" is the word "hate," you can clarify how you are using the word "love" in your argument. Often we better understand a topic by exploring what it is like (synonym) and what it is not like (antonym).

Another helpful definition technique is to provide a **procedural** or **operational definition**. This type of definition actually describes how something happens or occurs. For instance, words like "democracy" or "education," which can include concepts that are difficult to explain with just a simple definition, might be better illustrated by an explanation of how they are done or accomplished.

Now that you understand how to define terms appropriately, let's formulate a thesis statement for the curfew debate. As mentioned before, your parents' working definition of curfew is: "A rule that requires you to be in your house, or a previously approved house, by 10:00 p.m." You know that you want a more relaxed curfew. Your conclusion is that you want to be able to be in your home or a previously approved home by 12:00 a.m., and you want to be able to earn more privileges if you act responsibly within the initial guidelines your parents set. You believe that this will allow you more freedom, and it will allow you to practice responsibility. Therefore, you could frame your thesis statement like this: "A negotiable, 12:00 a.m. weekend curfew can help a young adult learn responsibility." Notice that this sentence can be proven true or false, which means it is debatable.

At this point, you know what logic is, you understand the importance of approaching any debate with humility, and you know how to define your position and its important terms. In the following chapter, you will learn about a few fallacies that people fall into as they are defining terms, and then you will be ready to form the main part of your curfew argument.

DEFINE

1. Thesis Statement:

2. Etymology:

3. Genus:

4. Species:

5. Description:

6. Example:

ANSWER

Explain why it is so important to establish a clear thesis statement and to define the key terms of your argument.

1. Genus and Species

a. Love

Genus: emotion

Species: happiness, hate, fear, excitement, sadness, elation

b. Speech

Genus: ____________________

Species: ____________________

c. Car

Genus: ____________________

Species: ____________________

d. Sister

Genus: ____________________

Species: ____________________

e. Buddhism

Genus: ____________________

Species: ____________________

PRACTICE

Determining the genus and species of a word can be tricky, so here is an opportunity to practice this helpful definition technique. First, under genus, write down the large category into which the word fits. Then, under species, list several other species that also fit in that larger category. A word may fit into several different genera (more than one genus), but in this case, just choose one. The first one has been done for you.

2. Etymology

For example, the word "faux pas" is French for "false step." In France, a faux pas can refer to either the use of bad grammar or to physical clumsiness, such as when someone trips. However, when English speakers use the term "faux pas," they are referring to actions or speech that violate common, but unspoken, social norms or traditions. When used in this manner, a faux pas falls into the genus of "mistake." Other species in this genus are: presenting incorrect information, acting on a mistaken idea, making an unwise choice, or accidentally violating a rule or law.

peccadillo	ennui	faux pas	ambulatory
pellucid	portmanteau	obstacle	demonstrative
ludicrous	auxiliary	oratory	laborious

PRACTICE

Choose one of these words, research its dictionary definition and etymology, and write them both down in the space provided. In addition, write the genus and species of your term.

PRACTICE

Use the word you chose in the previous exercise and think of examples from life that illustrate that word. In the space provided, you can either list several examples that clearly illustrate the word you chose, or you can discuss one example in detail. To help you gather details for your example(s), you might want to think about the 5 Ws and 1 H (who, what, where, when, why, and how) related to your example.

3. Examples

PRACTICE

Find three synonyms and three antonyms for the word you have been exploring in exercises 2 and 3 of this section.

4. Synonyms and Antonyms

ANALYZE

The provided excerpts use the common topic of definitions. Read the excerpts and then answer the corresponding questions.

1. From Harold Ickes' speech "What Is an American?"

What constitutes an American? Not color nor race nor religion. Not the pedigree of his family nor the place of his birth. Not the coincidence of his citizenship. Not his social status nor his bank account. Not his trade nor his profession. An American is one who loves justice and believes in the dignity of man. An American is one who will fight for his freedom and that of his neighbor. An American is one who will sacrifice property, ease and security in order that he and his children may retain the rights of free men. An American is one in whose heart is engraved the immortal second sentence of the Declaration of Independence.

Americans have always known how to fight for their rights and their way of life. Americans are not afraid to fight. They fight joyously in a just cause.

We Americans know that freedom, like peace, is indivisible. We cannot retain our liberty if three-fourths of the world is enslaved. Brutality, injustice and slavery, if practiced as dictators would have them, universally and systematically, in the long run would destroy us as surely as a fire raging in our nearby neighbor's house would burn ours if we didn't help to put out his.

a. At the beginning of this speech, Harold Ickes uses a definition device that we did not really discuss in this chapter but that is, nevertheless, very simple and effective. What is this definition device? What could be the danger of using this definition device to the exclusion of others?

b. In the second part of the speech, what definition device does Ickes primarily use?

c. If you were adding another section to this speech, what is one other definition device that would be especially effective? Why would it be effective? What is one device that you think would be ineffective? Explain your answer.

ANALYZE

2. From Susan B. Anthony's speech "On Woman's Right to Suffrage"

Friends and fellow Citizens: I stand before you tonight under indictment for the alleged crime of having voted at the last presidential election, without having a lawful right to vote. It shall be my work this evening to prove to you that in thus voting, I not only committed no crime, but, instead, simply exercised my citizen's rights, guaranteed to me and all the United States citizens by the National Constitution, beyond the power of any State to deny.

The preamble of the Federal Constitution says:"We the people of the United States, in order to form a more perfect union, establish justice, insure domestic tranquility, provide for the common defense, promote the general welfare, and secure the blessing of liberty to ourselves and our posterity, do ordain and establish this Constitution for the United States of America."

It was we, the people; not we, the white male citizens; nor yet we, the male citizens; but we, the whole people, who formed the Union. And we formed it, not to give the blessing of liberty, but to secure them; not to the half of ourselves and the half of our posterity, but to the whole people—women as well as men. And it is a downright mockery to talk to women of their enjoyment of the blessings of liberty while they are denied the use of the only means of securing them provides by this democratic-republican government—the ballot.

For any State to make sex a qualification that must ever result in the disfranchisement [sic] of one entire half of the people is to pass a bill of attainder, or an ex post facto law, and is therefore a violation of the supreme law of the land. By it the blessings of liberty are forever withheld from women.... Webster, Worcester, and Bouvier all define a citizen to be a person in the United States, entitled to vote and hold office. The only question left to be settled now is: Are women persons? And I hardly believe any of our opponents will have the hardihood to say they are not. Being person, then, women are citizens; and no State has a right to make any law, or to enforce an old law, that shall abridge their privileges or immunities. Hence, every discrimination against women in the constitutions and laws of the several States is to-day [sic] null and void, precisely as in every one against the negroes.[2]

a. What is Susan B. Anthony arguing for in this speech? Write her thesis in your own words.

____

____

____

____

____

b. In order to prove her point, Anthony defines several words. Below, list two of the words she defines.

____

____

____

____

ANALYZE

1. Continued

c. The term *ex post facto* law is a term in our constitution and would have been very familiar to people at that time, but is not necessarily familiar to people today. Find out what an *ex post facto* law is and then determine what Susan B. Anthony claims in her speech to be an *ex post facto* law.

ANALYZE

3. From Henry David Thoreau's "Walking"

I have met with but one or two persons in the course of my life who understood the art of Walking, that is, of taking walks—who had a genius, so to speak, for *sauntering*: which word is beautifully derived from "idle people who roved about the country, in the Middle Ages, and asked charity, under pretence of going *a la Sainte Terre*," to the Holy Land, till the children exclaimed, "There goes a *Sainte-Terrer*," a saunterer, a Holy-Lander. They who never go to the Holy Land in their walks, as they pretend, are indeed mere idlers and vagabonds; but they who do go there are saunterers in the good sense, such as I mean. Some, however, would derive the word from *sans terre*, without land or a home, which, therefore, in the good sense, will mean, having no particular home, but equally at home everywhere. For this is the secret of successful sauntering. He who sits still in a house all the time may be the greatest vagrant of all; but the saunterer, in the good sense, is not more vagrant than the meandering river, which is all the while sedulously seeking the shortest course to the sea. But I prefer the first, which, indeed, is the most probably definition. For every walk is a sort of crusade, preached by some Peter the Hermit in us, to go forth and reconquer this Holy Land from the hands of Infidels.

a. What is the key definition device that Thoreau uses in this passage?

b. The main topic of this essay is walking. However, Thoreau isn't just talking about walking as a means of getting from point A to point B, but rather his theme is focused more on walking as an experience. Write a paragraph in the space provided using the definition device of genus and species to add to this theme.

WRITE

Read the provided definition essay. Then, using the word you explored in the Practice section of the review exercises or one of the words listed here, write a similar definition paragraph. Be sure to use at least four of the definition techniques we have covered in this chapter.

freedom	integrity	patriotism
education	capital punishment	art

Sincerity is one of the most important characteristics a person can have if he wants to have good relationships with those around him. Webster's dictionary defines sincerity as "genuineness," "honesty," [or] "freedom from hypocrisy." *Sincere* comes from two Latin words: *sine*, meaning "without" and *cera* meaning "wax." So "sincere" literally means "without wax." This etymology may seem odd, but a brief story clearly illustrates this meaning. In Rome, there were many shops selling ornamental statues, and these statues were very popular. Sometimes, a statue maker would accidentally crack a statue as he was making it, but because he did not want to lose profit on this statue, he would seal the statue with wax and sell it to his customer without telling him of the cracks. This was unfair, however, because the customer was receiving damaged goods, while still paying the full price. Therefore, Roman shopkeepers began to post signs on their shops reading *Sincera*, which communicated to their customers that they were honest statue-makers, and they would not swindle their customers with damaged goods. Of course today, we do not associate statue-making with the word sincere, but it has retained its idea of honesty. Sincerity is a virtue, or a moral excellence, like prudence, temperance, justice, courage, and faithfulness. One of the most sincere people in history was Mother Theresa. She was completely honest in all of her dealings with people, whether they were poor lepers in India or presidents and other heads of countries that she met to discuss problems of poverty and other social issues. She was known for speaking directly and simply to people and showing compassion whether she went. Sincerity reflects solid, trustworthiness to people, and it lets them know they can trust you. Therefore, it helps build a great foundation for future friendships.

—Shelly Johnson

1. What is the dictionary definition of the word "uniform"?______________________________

2. What type of thing is a uniform? In other words, into what large category, or genus, does a uniform fit?

3. What are several other species in this genus? In other words, what other types of uniforms are there? How does a school uniform differ from other species in this genus?

4. What is the etymology of the word "uniform"?

5. Provide descriptions of uniforms you have seen in other organizational settings or in other schools.

6. What is one very clear example of a uniform in another school? Give as much detail as you can about it.

7. What are some words that could be synonyms for "uniform"? What words could be antonyms?

PREPARE

As you continue through this book, you will examine the curfew topic with each of the common topics. This will help you better understand how the common topics work. To provide you with additional practice with the common topics, you will also prepare for another debate, in which you will participate at the end of this book. For this debate, you will discuss the topic of school uniforms for junior high and high school students. In order to gather arguments for this debate, your class should determine what definition of "uniform" you will use. In order to do this, answer these questions about uniforms to help you determine the definition you want to use.

PREPARE

8. What is a procedural or operational definition for the word "uniform"? That is, how or why do schools use uniforms, and how do they work? ______________________________

Now that you have answered these questions, you can decide on the definition of uniform that you want to use as you debate this topic. Be sure to include answers to the following questions in your definition as you write it in the space provided:

- Will the uniform be one outfit that the students must wear each day, or will the uniform include several different outfit styles from which students can choose?
- Will the uniform be purchased from one specific vendor, or can students buy the uniform from any vendor as long as it meets the established uniform criteria?

PROPOSE

Now that you have determined what type of uniform you want to debate about, your teacher will split your class into two teams: one team will be for *the use of uniforms in junior and senior high schools, and the other team will be* against *it. Once you know whether you will be arguing for or against uniforms, write a thesis statement for your debate. Remember to form your conclusion into a declarative sentence that can be proven true or false.*

Congratulations! You now understand the first common topic and the most important part of debate: determining your thesis statement and defining your key terms. Now we need to look at several common mistakes people make when defining terms. These mistakes are **vagueness**, **ambiguity** and the fallacies of **equivocation** and **amphiboly**. If you understand each of these definition errors and learn to avoid them in your own arguments, you will be much more persuasive and clear. First, we will review what a fallacy is, and then we will examine each of the fallacies of definition.

In chapter 1, I mentioned that "fallacies" are "commonly recognized bad arguments." In other words, fallacies are errors in reasoning. To better understand this, let's review the two parts of an argument: the premises and the conclusion. The conclusion of an argument is what you believe or what you are trying to prove. The premises of an argument are the pieces of evidence or the proof that you are giving to support your argument. If you construct a good argument, the premises, or the proof, should lead directly to the conclusion. Remember that when you construct an inductive argument, the premises will not lead directly to the conclusion the way that deductive premises do in deductive arguments. However, if your inductive argument is well-formed, the premises will lead to the conclusion closely enough to warrant an **inductive leap**. When people make an inductive leap, they accept the conclusion of an inductive argument because the premises are believable, they provide ample proof for the conclusion, and it is reasonable to accept the conclusion. For example, let us consider again the inductive study we addressed in chapter 1 regarding smoking and lung cancer. A medical researcher studying the link between smoking and lung cancer surveys 5,000 smokers, and finds that 4,988 of the smokers have lung cancer. Although this evidence does not *absolutely* prove that smoking causes lung cancer, the premises provide enough evidence to warrant an inductive leap. So, when your argument contains valid premises, they will lead to a valid conclusion. However, when you commit a fallacy, your premises do not lead to your conclusion.

Now that you understand why committing fallacies can cause you to present an erroneous argument, let's look specifically at fallacies of definition. To understand the first two fallacies, we need to understand two problems that can lead to these fallacies: vagueness and ambiguity. When a word is vague, it is unclear, fuzzy, or imprecise because it can have a wide range of meaning or intensity. Vagueness often also means that certain words have been used so much that they have lost their meaning. Words such as "nice," "good," "important," "thing," and "bad" are vague words. For example, you might refer to a poorly cooked meal, a terrible sickness, or a bloody war in another country as "bad." It is a fuzzy, "loose" word that can be used to describe a variety of situations. This may seem like a good quality, but a word like this doesn't mean much because it can mean anything. It is better to avoid vague words like this because they are unclear and can be interpreted in different ways.

For example, the thesis statement "Capital punishment is bad" can be confusing. For whom is it bad? For whom is it good? Do you mean "bad" as in painful, or morally wrong, or bad for society? In order to argue about a topic like this, you need to use a much more precise word than "bad." The following are some possible alternative thesis statements for an argument *against* capital punishment:

Capital punishment is unethical.

Capital punishment fails to stop crime.

Capital punishment is state-sanctioned revenge.

If you wanted to argue *for* capital punishment, you might use one of these thesis statements:

Capital punishment is a form of justice.

Capital punishment is a biblical commandment.

Capital punishment stops crime.

When you use precise words in your thesis statement, you avoid vagueness, and you are able to address your topic more effectively.

When you use precise words in your thesis statement, you avoid vagueness, and you are able to address your topic more effectively. When people are vague in their arguments, they do not necessarily commit a fallacy, but they create an opportunity for misunderstanding.

Another problem of definition, ambiguity, can cause confusion just as vagueness can. Ambiguity occurs not because a word could have a range of meanings, but because it has several different common meanings, and it is not clear which one is being used. For instance, the word "plane" might refer to a flat or level surface or to a transportation vehicle. The word "cool" can mean "cold," or it can be used as a popular expression of approval. These words can be ambiguous because they can express different ideas depending upon the context in which they are used. Phrases can also be ambiguous.

There are two fallacies of ambiguity that people commit: equivocation and amphiboly. Let's look at a common example of the fallacy of equivocation. You may be aware that for the last couple of decades one of the greatest debates in our society has been over the teaching of evolution in school. This debate is especially heated because people on one side of the argument believe that evolution is scientific fact, and, therefore, that it would be irresponsible not to teach it in school. On the other side of the debate, there are people who believe that evolution is not fact and that it contradicts basic religious truth. Unfortunately, when people debate about this topic, they can confuse one another because the term "evolution" is ambiguous and can refer to several different concepts. In other words, people often commit the fallacy of equivocation when discussing this topic. When a person commits this fallacy, he argues as though he is using a single of definition of a term, but he is actually using more than one definition.

For instance, the word "evolution" can mean the broad concept of "change over time." Everyone accepts this type of evolution as true. After all, it is easily observed: people change over time, landscapes change over time, and even languages change over time. However, besides this broad definition of evolution, there are also several other types of evolution to which people discussing the topic of evolution could be referring. There is "micro-evolution,"

which can be defined as change within a species. Such a change could be when the color of an animal's skin or fur changes over time to adapt to an environmental change. "Macro-evolution," on the other hand, is a change from one species to another, such as if a reptile evolved into a bird, or a fish evolved into a mammal.[1] Two other common terms that people use in the discussion of evolution are "theistic evolution" and "naturalistic evolution." Theistic evolutionists believe that God or a Creator used evolution to create the world. Naturalistic evolutionists believe that the process of evolution is unguided and random and that there is no God or Supreme Being behind it.[2] Therefore, because there are so many different terms within the topic of evolution, it is easy for people to equivocate and confuse each other when they are discussing this important subject. For instance, a person might discuss the evidence for micro-evolution and then later use the same evidence to validate macro-evolution. However, macro-evolution is very different from micro-evolution, so using the same evidence could be both misleading and confusing. This is an example of equivocation. To avoid equivocation it is crucial that you define the key words in your topic and then consistently use those definitions throughout your debate.

The story of the *Odyssey* offers a classic example of the second fallacy of ambiguity: amphiboly. You may recall that Odysseus, a Greek hero who was trying to reach his beloved island of Ithaca after the Trojan War, was trapped on an island in the cave of Cyclops and could not escape because the giant rolled a boulder in front of the cave entrance. After blinding Cyclops' one eye, Odysseus finally escaped. As he sailed away, Cyclops, tormented by pain, shouted out for Odysseus to reveal his name. Odysseus shouted back, "My name is 'No One.'" Later, Cyclops' friends asked who had blinded him, and Cyclops responded, "No One blinded me." This is a good example of amphiboly. The phrase "No One blinded me" can be taken in two ways, which is what Odysseus was certainly counting on. It could either mean that a person named "No One" blinded Cyclops or that "no person" blinded him. To deceive Cyclops, Odysseus used amphiboly, which is using the same phrase in two different ways.

In his book *Introduction to Logic*, Irving Copi presents another example of amphiboly from ancient literature. King Croesus of Lydia wanted to go to war with the king of Persia. As he did with many important decisions, Croesus decided to consult the oracle (a person who was said to communicate with the gods) at Delphi. The oracle prophesied to Croesus that if he went to war with Persia, a mighty kingdom would be destroyed. Emboldened by this favorable prophecy, Croesus waged a war with Persia and was utterly defeated. When Croesus complained to a priest of the Delphi Oracle, the priest responded that the oracle had spoken the truth: Croesus *had* destroyed a mighty kingdom—his own.[3]

You may have noticed that while it could be very easy to equivocate or use amphiboly accidentally, it is also possible to use these fallacies purposefully to deceive. These fallacies can be used as a verbal sleight-of-hand. By "sleight-of-hand," I am referring to the distracting tricks magicians use to focus your attention on one hand while they are tricking you with the other hand. Sometimes arguers will use amphiboly to trick you and take your attention from the main issue or from the weakness of their argument. Learning these fallacies of definition will help you avoid them in your own arguments and resist being tricked with them by other people.

DEFINE

1. Vagueness: ______

2. Ambiguity: ______

3. Equivocation: ______

4. Amphiboly: ______

IDENTIFY

Each of the provided statements contains an italicized term or phrase that is vague or ambiguous. In the space provided, explain how each phrase or word could be understood in two different ways.

Errors of Equivocation and Amphiboly

1. After attending a dinner party, my roommate told me that he enjoyed a good *punch* on a warm summer's evening. Therefore, around the same time the next evening, I punched him in the nose.

2. A little boy who was terrified of *bats* refused to go into the barn of his family's farm at night because of the bats there. To play a cruel joke on him, his older brothers blindfolded him and told him they had a surprise for him. They led him into the barn that night, at which point they made screeching bat noises. The little boy ran screaming out of the barn and went directly to his mother. When the mother scolded the other brothers, they said, in feigned innocence, that they thought it would be OK because no one was playing baseball in the barn that night.

IDENTIFY

3. A man named Al wanted to purchase a new car, and, in order to save money, he visited a used car lot. After looking at several cars, one of the salesmen showed Al his dream car at an incredible price. Al, who was a little naïve, exclaimed, "What a great car! What a great price! Can this be possible?" The salesman responded to him, "*Let's just say that if you buy this car, there will be one more very happy person in this world!*" Al was so excited that he bought the car immediately. On his way to work the next day, Al's new car broke down, and he discovered that it was unfixable. Al returned to the salesman and accused him, saying, "You lied to me. You said that if I bought this car, there would be one more very happy person in this world! Well, my car broke down, I can't fix it, and I am certainly not happy!" The salesman looked innocently at Al, and replied, "But my dear sir! When I said that there would be one more very happy person in the world, I meant me. I have been trying to get rid of that car for months, and now, thanks to you, I am a very happy man, indeed!"

DETERMINE

The provided humorous sentences are actual phrases or announcements that were in church bulletins. Note in the space provided whether the errors in these sentences are equivocation or amphiboly.[4]

Humor with Fallacies

1. For those of you who have children and don't know it, we have a nursery downstairs.

2. The eighth graders will be presenting Shakespeare's *Hamlet* in the church basement on Friday at 7 p.m. The congregation is invited to attend the tragedy.

3. This being Easter Sunday, we will ask Mrs. Lewis to come forward and lay an egg on the altar.

4. The preacher will preach his farewell massage, after which the choir will sing, "Break Forth With Joy."

5. The Rev. Merriweather spoke briefly, much to the delight of the audience.

6. Next Sunday Mrs. Vinson will be soloist for the morning service. The pastor will then speak on "It's a Terrible Experience."

WRITE

Fortunetellers often provide their customers with ambiguous statements that seem to promise a great future. Modeling your story along the pattern of the story of Croesus and the Delphic Oracle, write a short story about a person who runs into a conflict with a local fortuneteller. Make sure that the story hinges around an ambiguous statement given by the fortuneteller, just like that of the Delphic Oracle and the used car dealer in the example about Al and his used car misfortune.

Ambiguity and Creative Writing

REWRITE

Each of the provided thesis statements has a vague term that is italicized. Rewrite the statement, replacing the vague term with a more precise term or phrase.

1. Studying is a *good* habit.

2. Exercising regularly is *helpful*.

3. Being friendly to people is *good*.

4. Gossip is *bad*.

5. Helping little old ladies across the street is *right*.

EXAMINE

Now that you understand the problems of vagueness and ambiguity, you need to examine the thesis statement for the uniform debate you wrote in the previous chapter. Is it clear? Are any of your terms vague or ambiguous? Could they be misunderstood by a person with whom you were discussing this topic? If so, rewrite the statement in the provided space so that it is free from any of these problems.

Your Debate Thesis Statement

Common Topic 2

Testimony

The common topic of testimony is one of the most important and useful common topics you will ever use because it draws on the experience and opinion of other people. If you think about it, we often base decisions or choices on the advice of trusted friends and family members. The following subtopics of testimony represent different ways in which we can use the experience of other people in our arguments. There are also fallacies listed with most of the subtopics.

Examples (also known as **precedent**): When we use the subtopic of example, we look to the past to figure out what to do. By noticing how life works, or seeing the results of peoples' decisions, we can understand how to act. Whenever we use examples, we must be careful not to make a hasty generalization, which is a conclusion based on an atypical example.

Authority (also referred to as **expert opinion**): People such as scientists, professors, doctors, lawyers, etc., can be considered experts, or authorities, on certain topics. Because it is not possible to do thorough research on every topic you want to know about, experts are often consulted to find out the truth about different matters. Consulting authorities can be a timesaving habit. However, it is important that these authorities actually are authorities on the topic you are researching. If you rely on the testimony of a person who is testifying out of his or her field of expertise, you might commit the fallacy of **illegitimate appeal to authority**

Statistics: Statistics is the "branch of mathematics dealing with the collection, analysis, interpretation, and presentation of masses of numerical data." To examine how statistics work in real life, let's say that we are a research group that wants to determine how effective a new medicine is. We might survey thousands of people that have taken this medicine. If it was effective in eighty-five percent of cases, we would probably think it was successful; if it was only effective in fifteen percent, we would not think it was successful. With statistics, usually the higher or lower the percentage, the more significant the findings. Statistics can be convincing because they are a scientific tool. However, you must be careful when you use and read statistics because people can easily use them to lie. In fact, an entire book—*How to Lie with Statistics*—was written about doing just that. Later, we will examine how people do, in fact, lie with statistics.

Furthermore, we must take the words of an authority in context, rather than misrepresenting his words or misapplying them to an irrelevant situation. When we take a person's words out of context to make them mean something different than their original meaning, we are committing the fallacy of **accent**.

Proverbs: Throughout history, wise people have said memorable and insightful things about a wide variety of topics. For example, some of our most common sayings, such as "The early bird catches the worm," come from famous and intelligent people, such as Ben Franklin. Using wise sayings can effectively illustrate an argument, but you must avoid the fallacy of **clichéd thinking**. Proverbs are meant to illustrate general truths, and therefore are not ironclad rules or mathematical formulas that are applicable to every situation. If you try to apply them in that manner, you are misusing them and you will likely appear ridiculous or stale and boring.

Testimonial: A testimonial can be defined as a firsthand account of something a person has experienced, When we consult a person's testimonial we are learning about the experience of a person who is like us. This person is not necessarily an expert, but because of what she has experienced, she might be able to provide helpful information on a specific topic. Testimonials can be enlightening, but we must remember that the people giving them may not be using good logic, their success may be short-lived, or they may even be lying or exaggerating about their experience. It is also important to realize that one example very rarely is sufficient to prove a point.

With the subtopic of testimonial, it is important to avoid the fallacy of **bandwagon**. When people commit the fallacy of bandwagon, they argue that because everyone believes something or does something, then it must be true or the right thing to do. While something believed or done by a large group of people, particularly wise and mature people, may be true, history shows that there have been many times when large groups of people have done or believed very wrong things.

In the next several chapters, we will discover the subtopics that fall under the common topic of testimony. This common topic will most likely be the one you use most often; therefore, it is especially wise to learn how to use this common topic well.

Chapter 5 *Subtopic: Examples*

All people use rules and principles to guide their lives. For many, these rules and principles come from their religious beliefs and morals. Other principles are passed down from important people, like parents or other family members. People also form many of the rules for their lives just by observing life. You do this all the time. For instance, if you believe you need to study hard to get good grades, you have probably observed your friends, older brothers and sisters, and maybe even your parents studying hard to achieve good grades. By observing the examples set by others, you've decided that studying hard produces worthy results.

As another example, consider a common piece of wisdom by which you live: "Look both ways before crossing the street." Do you believe this is a good rule because something terrible happens to you whenever you don't look both ways before you cross the street? Certainly not. Sometimes there are no cars approaching when you cross the street, so you could proceed blindly across the road without injury. However, you have most likely observed or heard of people who received serious injuries because they crossed the street without looking. Therefore, because of these examples, which you could have witnessed from everyday life, you have adopted the rule: "Look both ways before you cross the road." When you reason by example, you observe life, notice a pattern, and form generalizations on that pattern.

In order to construct good arguments from example, you must adopt several important guidelines. First, you should pick a variety of examples from different sources with which you will illustrate your point. Providing only one example, however interesting it may be, certainly doesn't prove anything. For instance, let us say that a man named Peter wants to prove that people who read voraciously get excellent jobs. He might give an example of a friend named Bob who reads a book every day and who has a very good job. However, this does not *prove* Peter's point. It is an interesting example, and might cause us to consider his argument, but it is not enough proof.

Let's say Peter strengthens his argument and demonstrates that Bob has eight brothers and sisters who read a book every day and they all have wonderful jobs. These examples are still problematic. Perhaps all of the people in Bob's family are also extremely skilled business people, and therefore a person could argue that it is the business skills of Bob's family, rather than their voracious reading, that earned them their excellent jobs. However, if Peter can produce examples of voracious readers with excellent jobs throughout history from all over the world, that would strengthen his thesis. When a widespread phenomenon occurs consistently over a lengthy period of time, we begin to note patterns. Because of this, it is wise for you to use a wide variety of examples from a wide variety of sources to support your point.

It is not always possible or necessary for you to list a host of different examples to prove your point. When you argue casually with friends and family, or if you are writing a short essay, it is not possible to list dozens of examples. In these cases, using a couple of well-chosen examples and perhaps some other arguments taken from other common topics will help you construct a good argument. However, the longer and more complex your argument is, the larger the number and greater the variety of examples you should use.

Second, you must carefully examine the background information of the examples you use. For instance, consider again Peter's argument about people who read a great deal. Imagine that he has another friend named Rachel who has an excellent job and who claims to be a voracious reader. When Peter examines Rachel's reading habits further, however, he discovers that although Rachel thinks she reads a lot, she actually only reads one book a year. Obviously this would not be a good example for Peter to use to support his argument. Sometimes it might seem like an example supports an argument well, but upon further examination, it actually does not. Therefore, it is always important for people to examine their examples thoroughly to make sure they are solid.

Third, you must consider **counterexamples**. A counterexample is an example that seems to disprove or contradict an arguer's thesis. For instance, imagine that, during his research, Peter discovers that some people who do not read at all have excellent jobs. At first, Peter might be inclined to ignore these counterexamples and focus only on the examples that help prove his point. However, his opponents might present these counterexamples later, and if Peter has not carefully considered the counterexamples so that he can refute them, his argument could be damaged.

If you want to use good logic, you must be willing to admit that your thesis may be wrong.

You might wonder what you should do if you find counterexamples that contradict your thesis. There are two options. First, if you want to use good logic, you must be willing to admit that your thesis may be wrong. If you decide, at the beginning of the argument, that your thesis is infallible, you might ignore relevant evidence that will help you discover the truth or make it easy for your opponent to refute your conclusion. If you decide that your thesis is wrong, you may need to change it or admit to your opponent that you were mistaken in your views. You may think that this is a sign of failure, but being willing to consider both sides of an issue and to change your views if the evidence demands it is actually a sign of thorough, logical thinking. Second, you must realize that counterexamples do not automatically destroy an argument. Sometimes, as you research the counterexample, you will find that it does not actually refute your thesis. For instance, suppose that Peter examines the group of non-readers with excellent jobs. It may be that these people have not read any books over the last two years, but they usually read a great deal. This actually supports Peter's thesis, rather than contradicting it.

Furthermore, counterexamples are sometimes **anomalies**. Anomalies are exceptions or odd occurrences that don't fit a normal pattern. Almost any pattern or rule has an exception. One or two exceptions do not disprove a general rule. For instance, imagine that Peter surveys 10,000 people, and of those 10,000 people, 98 percent of those who read regularly have good jobs. We can conclude that the remaining two percent are an anomaly and that, generally, people who read a lot do have good jobs. (You might be wondering at this point if it is really true that people who read a lot of books get good jobs. I am not

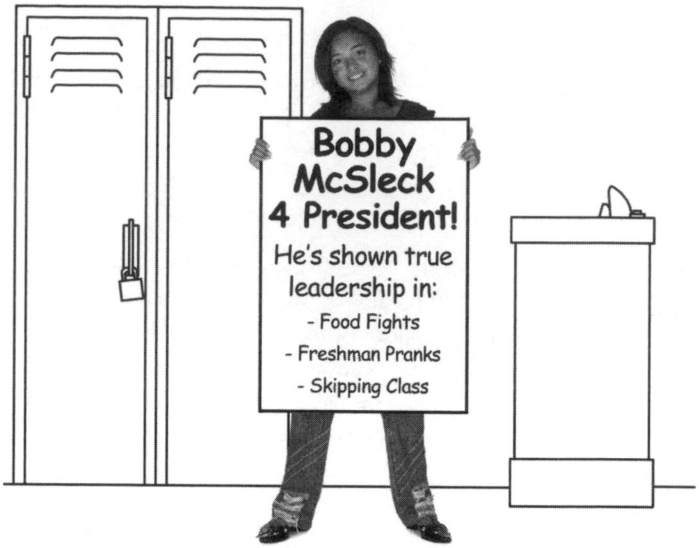

sure if there are actually any studies on this particular idea. However, research exists which indicates that better-educated people have higher-paying jobs. For more on this, see the exercises in chapter 6, which covers the subtopic of statistics).

Another type of example that is used in arguments is **precedent**. By using a precedent in an argument, you are referring to the past to support a claim or interpretation in the present. For instance, if you believe that it is important to be kind to others, you probably believe this because your parents have taught you this. You probably also believe this because, in the past, you have noticed examples of people who treat others with kindness, and you have decided that, generally, people who act this way get along with others better and have more friends. When you reason in this manner, you are using precedent. That is, in the past you noticed a pattern of behavior that achieved positive results (being kind to others results in good relationships), and that observation now governs how you relate to people. Another form of this type of example is the **legal precedent**, which is a legal decision that sets a pattern or establishes a principle or rule that a court adopts when deciding later cases that have similar issues or facts. When a judge or a lawyer examines a case, he or she considers examples of past similar cases in order to determine a present course of action. For most of your arguments, you will not examine past legal cases, although you might for debates in which you are proposing a change in national policy or law. In a situation like the curfew debate, you can use a form of legal precedent by discussing other rules, past and present, which pertain to the rule you are discussing.

Speaking of the curfew debate, let's look at it a little more closely and consider what examples might prove enlightening. Remember that at this point you have decided that you want to argue for a negotiable 12:00 a.m. weekend curfew. To support this argument, it would help you if you could find several examples of teenagers who benefit from such a curfew. When we examined definition techniques, we discussed your friend, David, and his lenient curfew. This example would be especially helpful if David is a responsible, mature teenager whom your parents respect. You should also look for examples of situations in which teenagers are significantly disadvantaged by a strict curfew. Perhaps the teenagers' parents are overprotective, causing the teenagers to miss out on valuable activities. Or perhaps a strict curfew causes constant tension within a family.

To be fair, you should also examine counterexamples. For instance, you might examine examples of teenagers who benefit from strict curfews or suffer from lenient curfews. Remember that these counterexamples do not automatically disprove your thesis. There might be other reasons, irrelevant to your thesis, why a strict curfew is positive and a lenient curfew is detrimental in some situations. For example, perhaps it is not the curfew that causes problems, but certain family dynamics instead. When you encounter anomalies, keep an open mind and continue researching.

As you read the rest of this book, you will learn that examples are the foundation for many of the other common topics. For instance, the common topic of comparison demonstrates similarities between two examples, and the common topic of relationship examines causal connections between examples. Because arguments from example are the foundation of inductive arguments, you will often apply these rules to other argument techniques.

DEFINE

1. Example: ______

2. Anomaly: ______

3. Counterexample: ______

4. Precedent: ______

READ & ANSWER

Arguments from Examples: Read the provided arguments from examples and answer the questions following each of them.

1. Hebrews 11:1-8, NASB

Now faith is the assurance of things hoped for, the conviction of things not seen. For by it the men of old gained approval.

By faith we understand the worlds were prepared by the word of God, so that what is seen was not made out of things which are visible. By faith, Abel offered to God a better sacrifice than Cain, through which he obtained the testimony that he was righteous, God testifying about his gifts, and through faith, though he is dead, he still speaks. By faith Enoch was taken up so that he should not see death; AND HE WAS NOT FOUND BECAUSE GOD TOOK HIM UP; for he obtained the witness that before his being taken up he was pleasing to God. And without faith it is impossible to please Him, for he who comes to God must believe that He is and that He is a rewarder of those who seek Him. By faith Noah, being warned by God about things not yet seen, in reverence prepared an ark for the salvation of his household, by which he condemned the world, and became an heir of the righteousness which is according to faith.

By faith Abraham, when he was called, obeyed by going out to a place which he was to receive for an inheritance; and he went out, not knowing where he was going.

a. What is the thesis of these verses? Write it in your own words.

______

READ & ANSWER

1. Continued

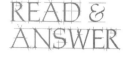

b. Think of two other biblical examples that support this thesis and explain why they are good examples.

READ & ANSWER

2. Francis Bacon's "Of Empire"

It is a miserable state of mind, to have few things to desire, and many things to fear; and yet that commonly is the case of kings; who, being at the highest, want matter of desire, which makes their minds more languishing; and have many representations of perils and shadows, which makes their minds the less clear.

And this is one reason also, of that effect which the Scripture speaketh of, That the king's heart is inscrutable. For multitude of jealousies, and lack of some predominant desire, that should marshal and put in order all the rest, maketh any man's heart, hard to find or sound. Hence it comes likewise, that princes many times make themselves desires, and set their hearts upon toys; sometimes upon a building; sometimes upon erecting of an order; sometimes upon the advancing of a person; sometimes upon obtaining excellency in some art, or feat of the hand; as Nero for playing on the harp, Domitian for certainty of the hand with the arrow, Commodus for playing at fence, Caracalla for driving chariots, and the like. This seemeth incredible, unto those that know not the principle, that the mind of man, is more cheered and refreshed by profiting in small things, than by standing at a stay, in great. We see also that kings that have been fortunate conquerors, in their first years, it being not possible for them to go forward infinitely, but that they must have some check, or arrest in their fortunes, turn in their latter years to be superstitious, and melancholy; as did Alexander the Great; Diocletian; and in our memory, Charles the Fifth; and others: for he that is used to go forward, and findeth a stop, falleth out of his own favor, and is not the thing he was.[1]

a. Put Francis Bacon's thesis in your own words. (His wording is a little unusual, so read it again carefully if you have trouble comprehending his prose. His true thesis is implied in the second paragraph, toward the end.) You may have noticed that Bacon seems to have a second thesis, or main point, at the end of the second paragraph. What is it?

b. Where are the examples that Bacon gives to support his point? ______

READ & ANSWER

3. Shelly Johnson's "Dictators and Anarchy"

There is a truth observed in history that dictators often arise when there is a great deal of economic chaos and disaster. For instance, in ancient Rome before Rome became an empire, it suffered from a series of civil wars. Many war generals tried to seize Rome. Finally, Julius Caesar, another war general, came to the throne, and although he was later assassinated, he established a dictatorship (as an emperor) that lasted many years. In modern times, Hitler became powerful after Germany had been devastated by World War I. The Germans were demoralized and faced severe economic crisis. When Hitler promised to restore the former glory of Germany, he was able to gain supreme power.

In addition, many South American countries that have had the greatest amount of unrest and chaos also have had some of the strongest dictatorships. In conclusion, times of economic crisis seem to produce the perfect condition for the rise of powerful, and often cruel, dictators.

READ & ANSWER

a. State the thesis of this excerpt in your own words. ______

b. Find an example and a counterexample to my thesis. Is the counterexample you found a true counterexample or an anomaly? Explain your answer. ______

CRITIQUE

These three arguments all use examples to discuss the following saying: "You reap what you sow." Read each argument twice and then choose which one you feel presents the strongest points, being sure to describe why you think it is the best argument. Then write an assessment of the good and bad points of the arguments you considered not quite as strong.

When using examples to persuade an audience, remember the following rules or guidelines:

- Use a wide variety of examples from many different sources.
- Check background information.
- Carefully consider counterexamples.

1. In the Old Testament we read about a king named Saul who also reaped what he sowed. During the early part of his reign, Saul was described as a valiant, good, God-fearing king. Slowly and increasingly, however, Saul began to disregard God's commands and even sought to kill David, an upright man who later succeeded Saul as king. Later, because of his wickedness and corruption, Saul went mad, and he was eventually killed in battle. The infamous Goliath also illustrates the principle that you reap what you sow. Goliath the Philistine, was a bloodthirsty, merciless warrior who himself died without mercy when the youthful David killed him with a slingshot and then cut off his head.

In our own time, Mussolini and Hitler present perfect examples of this adage. Both of these men led extremely violent lives, killing thousands of people in wars and purges. Not suprisingly, they also died violent deaths.

2. The old saying, "You reap what you sow" has a lot of truth in it. For instance, I know this bully at school named Alf who was always mean to kids, and finally he got suspended. Another bully in the fifth grade tripped a boy in the hall, and he had to stay after school for detention.

3. There is a great deal of truth in the saying, "You reap what you sow." For example, in *Macbeth*, Macbeth and Lady Macbeth conspired to assassinate their king, Duncan. Later, both of them went mad and died violent deaths. In *Hamlet*, Claudius murdered his brother and the king so that he could get the throne, and later, he was killed by Hamlet. Lastly, in *King Lear*, Goneril and Regan are greedy and cruel to their father. In the end, Goneril poisons her sister and then murders herself. These examples clearly show that a person reaps what he sows.

It is true that some evil people do not seem to reap what they sow. There are some evil people who seem to prosper despite their wickedness. However, usually these people are not as happy as they may seem and suffer some evil consequences for their cruelty. For instance, Henry VIII divorced and killed many wives. Although he did not die a terrible death, he did miss out on the peaceful, marital happiness that comes from a long and faithful marriage. In addition, although he desperately wanted a son, he only had one, and that son died at a very young age.

DEVELOP

Now that you are more familiar with arguments from example, develop some arguments from this subtopic that support your thesis statement for the uniform debate. Use the provided questions to help you, and then write a paragraph supporting your argument. Include at least three relevant examples and one counterexample. Remember that unless your counterexample has influenced you to change your thesis statement, you should explain why it really isn't a counterexample after all.

Dress Codes and Arguments from Example

1. If you support the use of uniforms in school, can you think of other schools in which uniforms have been a positive influence? Can you think of other non-academic environments benefited by uniforms? ______________________________

2. If you do not support the use of uniforms in school, can you think of other school situations in which uniforms have produced negative effects? Can you think of non-academic environments hindered by uniforms? ______________________________

3. Think of at least two counterexamples to your thesis statement. How do you explain these counterexamples? Unless you are persuaded by your counterexample to change your thesis, you should explain why the counterexamples are anomalous or irrelevant. ______________________________

Arguments using statistics are extremely common today. For instance, you may hear a commercial boasting that nine out of ten doctors recommend a certain medicine or that a medicine is effective eighty-eight percent of the time. A statistic is a number that represents a large quantity of examples. Statistics can be powerful because they represent dozens or even hundreds and thousands of examples.

You may remember that in the last chapter, I suggested that when using the subtopic of examples it is wise to use many examples from a variety of places and situations. Let's say that a drug manufacturer was trying to prove that a new drug called Solacile effectively relieves the symptoms of depression. During the testing of the drug, several thousand people tried Solacile, and most of them experienced significant relief from their depression symptoms, leading the drug company to become very optimistic about the drug. Furthermore, let's assume that the company received approval from the FDA to sell Solacile, and now the company is ready to start an advertising and promotion campaign.

The chief marketing agent at the company could promote Solacile several different ways. He could ask dozens of the study participants to write a short paragraph describing the effectiveness of the drug so that he could publish those testimonials in an advertisement. In fact, many researchers or companies do this when they are advertising a new product. However, because many people will most likely not take the time to read all of the testimonials, the marketing agent might instead publish a statistic like this: "Ninety-five percent of people who took Solacile for depression experienced significant relief from their depression symptoms after one week." In this way, he quickly demonstrates the effectiveness of Solacile.

Because statistics seem scientific, they can be extremely convincing. However, it is easy to manipulate statistics in such a way that you can prove, or seem to prove, almost anything. For instance, what if I told you that through recent research, I had discovered that wearing purple is dangerous? I could report that eighty-five percent of people in my study who wore purple had been struck with hard objects, which resulted in some type of bruising. This would sound strange and alarming until you learned that the people in my "study" were all on the girls' volleyball team of a local high school—a team that wears purple uniforms. They had been struck with hard objects because they habitually play intense volleyball. The hard object that struck them was the volleyball, and all of the players on the team made contact with the ball in some manner because they were serving, setting, bumping, and spiking, which typically results in bruises on their arms. Once you learn the nature of the research behind this statistic, you can see that it is a deceptive, misleading statistic because of the small and abnormal research sample of a girl's volleyball team that wears purple uniforms.

How do you know that the statistics you want to use are accurate and meaningful? You need to examine the **sample** of the study. The sample is the group of people or examples the researchers tested to form their statistic. This group typically represents a picture of the general population. In the example of Solacile, the sample was the hundreds or thousands of people who tried Solacile.

Generally, when you use statistics, the larger and more randomly selected the sample, the better it is. Since the sample used for the "purple is dangerous" research was a very small sample, and was not very randomly selected, it would not support an argument well.

Let's further examine the importance of using a large sample that is randomly selected. For example, in my "purple is dangerous" study, I based my statistic only on people wearing purple on the volleyball team at a local school, which was a sample size of ten to fifteen girls. If I had surveyed thousands of purple-wearing people from all over the United States, I would have discovered significantly different results. The smaller your sample is, the more likely it is that there is some other factor common to the sample group that influences the outcome. The larger the sample, the less probable it is that there is some other factor affecting all of the people in the sample.

In order to consider the idea of random sampling, let's revisit the Solacile study. In order for this study to be truly authentic, the researchers should randomly pick a large group of people to try the drug. When you use a **random sample**, it means that one person in the study has no more chance than another to be chosen for the study.[1] If you do not choose people randomly, you choose them from a special group or you choose them using a pre-determined pattern. For instance, if you put the name of every single person in the United States in a very large hat, and you choose 5,000 individuals from that hat, you are choosing people randomly. However, if a researcher chooses a sample of people from his family, church, or neighborhood, that is not random. Non-random samples are not as reliable as random samples.

For example, with the Solacile study, if the researcher picked depressed people from his neighborhood or church to try the drug, there might be some other common factor, besides Solacile, that relieved their depression. For instance, if the people were all in the same family, they might be more depressed in the winter but happier in the summer. If all of the people were in the same church, their pastor might have preached a series of sermons on hope, which lifted their depression during the research period. If people are picked randomly for a study, there is less chance that there will be some outside, common factor influencing the research.

Unfortunately, people often place too much trust in claims that *sound* scientific. Science is extremely valuable and has solved dilemmas throughout history, but scientists are humans and they can make mistakes. In fact, it is not uncommon for researchers to publish a theory one year, and then publish another study the following year that contradicts the previous theory. If you have heard or read about diet research, you may have observed this phenomenon. Some researchers say that eating a lot of protein and fewer carbohydrates is the best diet. Others say that eating less protein and more carbohydrates is the best diet. Others report that following a low-fat diet is the answer, and still others will claim that low-fat diets actually make people fat. This doesn't mean that science and statistics are worthless. On the contrary, they can certainly help us search for truth. However, when using or listening to statistics, realize that people can use statistics deceptively and that studies can be flawed. Therefore, you need to use the skills you are learning to analyze these studies, rather than putting immediate and complete trust in them.

DEFINE

1. Statistics: ______

2. Sample: ______

3. Random Sample: ______

ANSWER

1. Why is it important to use a large, random sample to achieve a reliable study? ______

2. How could someone lie with statistics? ______

DETERMINE

To demonstrate how people can manipulate statistics, think of an outrageous claim you want to make. Then, determine a sample group to use that will demonstrate this conclusion.

Manipulating Statistics for Fun and Games:

ANALYZE

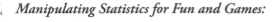

Research Studies: Read each of the statistical studies provided and answer the questions that follow.

Note: The following excerpt is from a book called *Failure to Connect: How Computers Affect Our Children's Minds—for Better and Worse*. The cited study attempted to determine whether students learn more when they use computer programs in the classroom rather than traditional tools. "LOGO" is a computer language, "CAI" is an acronym for "computer assisted instruction," and a "meta-analysis" is a technique researchers use to look at vast quantities of data to determine trends and patterns.[2]

> 1. James Kulik of the University of Michigan ran a meta-analysis of ninety-seven studies in elementary and high schools and found major discrepancies in the data. Some computerized instruction raised achievement scores, but some significantly lowered them. Kulik also found inconsistent results for LOGO (e.g., some studies showed gains in problem-solving skills, while others did not) and "little effect" on science learning from simulated programs. Most notable, when he compared CAI with the same amount of time spent with pencil, paper, and printed materials, the traditional materials did as well or better. Students tutored by fellow classmates scored almost as well as those tutored by computers.[3]

a. What was the sample in this study? Does it seem like it was a good sample size? Explain your answer.

ANALYZE

1. Continued

b. Does the excerpt tell us if the sample was random or not?

c. Summarize the findings of this study in your own words.

d. Should you base your opinion about computer-assisted learning on this study? Support your answer.

ANALYZE

2. The U.S. Department of Commerce, Bureau of the Census, "Current Population Report" reported these findings for the years 1990-2000:

- A male junior high school dropout earned $13,534 less per year than a high school graduate. In lifetime earnings, that amounts to $473,690.
- A male high school dropout earned $9,208 less annually than a high school graduate did. In lifetime earnings, that equates to $322,280.
- A male high school graduate earned $22,031 less annually than a college graduate did. In lifetime earnings, that equals $771,085.
- A female junior high school dropout earned $8,992 less per year than a high school graduate. That amounts to $314,720 in lifetime earnings.
- A female high school dropout earned $7,051 less annually than a high school graduate did. That equals $246,785 in lifetime earnings.
- A female high school graduate earned $15,445 less annually than a college graduate did. That equals $540,575 in lifetime earnings.[4]

a. Find out how the U.S. census is taken to determine whether or not this is a good sample. Explain your findings.

b. What are three trends or patterns that you notice from this data?

ANALYZE

2. Continued

c. Can you think of a counterexample to any of the trends here? How might this counterexample be explained? (If you need a hint, research how much schooling Bill Gates, founder of Microsoft, attained).

3. There is an interesting phenomenon that researchers have discovered called the "Hawthorne effect," which can make it difficult to obtain reliable statistics and data. This interesting excerpt describes it.

> The way in which subjects view a study and their participation in it can create a threat to [the reliability of the study]. One example is the well-known "Hawthorne effect," first observed in the Hawthorne plant of Western Electric Company some years ago. [During the study,] it was…discovered that productivity increased not only when improvements were made in physical working conditions (such as [an] increase in the number of coffee breaks and [the provision of] better lighting), but also when such conditions were unintentionally made worse (for instance, the number of coffee breaks was reduced and the lighting was dimmed). The…explanation [given] for this [phenomenon] is that the [workers perceived the changes in environment caused by the study as] special attention and recognition…; they felt someone cared about them and was trying to help them [even though some of the "attention" resulted in less-desirable working conditions. The term "Hawthorne effect" refers to this increase in productivity that occurs because subjects in a study perceive they are receiving more recognition and attention.][5]

a. Summarize the findings of this study.

ANALYZE

3. Continued

b. This excerpt does not directly state the sample group used in this study, but it implies it. Comment on the strength or weakness of this sample group.

c. If you wanted to further confirm the reality of this phenomenon, what are several steps you could take to do this?

RESEARCH

Now that you are more familiar with arguments made with statistics, take some time to research some studies for the uniform debate. Then write a paragraph about uniforms that has both a topic and concluding sentence that features at least one supporting statistic. Use available Internet and library sources to research this topic.

Arguments from Statistics and the Dress Code Debate

Chapter 7 *Subtopics: Authority, Proverbs, Testimonials, and Scripture*

In ancient times, it was possible to learn all of the known wisdom of that time. Today, because of the explosion of knowledge and technology, it is not possible to learn everything there is to know. That's where the subtopic of authority, or expert opinion, comes in. Because we can't know everything, we must consult other sources, such as experts or authorities, in order to find information on certain topics. By doing so, we benefit from the expertise of these other sources. How do we consult these experts? We read their books, watch their interviews on TV or on the Internet, listen to them on the radio, and interview them personally, if we can. Authorities are an invaluable resource, but it is important that we use this resource correctly.

To make sure that you are using an expert opinion, or authority, properly, you must first determine if an authority is actually an authority. To be an expert on a subject, a person must possess certain experience or credentials. For example, an expert in education might be a teacher who has taught for many years and who has thoroughly researched and experimented in a certain topic, such as successful strategies for teaching reading. He probably has a master's degree in some area of education. An expert on crime reduction may have been a lawyer, a psychologist or a law enforcement officer. She may have studied various causes of crime extensively and written a book about it. The point is, when you are using an authority to make an argument, make sure your authority actually has the qualifications and the knowledge to qualify him or her as an expert.

In addition, you must realize that although a person might be an authority in one field, he might address other topics about which he is not an expert. This doesn't mean that the person is automatically wrong, but it is important to recognize that the person is speaking out of his field of expertise. This occurs frequently in the world of advertising. Advertisers often use athletes to sell cars, or movie stars to sell food products. Usually these people have no special expertise in the products they are selling; however, the advertisers are hoping that consumers will associate these people's expertise in sports or acting (along with their cool reputation) with the product they are trying to sell. That is why you always need to analyze the supposed expertise of an authority, as well as the claims he makes. You should also critique his entire argument. To do this, determine the conclusion and the premises of the argument, and then analyze it for possible fallacies. Even though a person is an expert, he can still make mistakes, so you need to evaluate his argument using logic.

Proverbs, another subtopic of testimony, are an interesting type of argument. You have probably seen various quote books that contain the wise words of famous people on a variety of topics. For instance, earlier I mentioned one of Ben Franklin's sayings: "The early bird catches the worm." Another of Franklin's famous sayings is: "Do not put off until tomorrow what you can do today." If you look in a quote book, you will find many excellent sayings, or proverbs, written by people throughout history on hundreds of topics. Proverbs can be a good tool to use in arguments because they are often witty and thought provoking.

However, although proverbs are often written by famous people, those people are not necessarily experts on the topics they discuss. Many times, their words become famous because the people themselves are famous, and they use words cleverly. Therefore, although you can use proverbs with good effect in your debates, you should use them more as ornamentation, rather than as major support for your argument. For example, it is good to use them at the beginning or end of a speech or to highlight a previously developed idea. In addition, you need to realize that proverbs are generalizations, rather than ironclad rules. For instance, if you get up early every day to catch the proverbial "worm," you will notice that some days you catch it, and some days you don't. Proverbs are not formulas that always work, such as 2+2=4 does. They represent a general truth about life. When you try to apply them like a rule or formula, you are falling into a fallacy called "clichéd thinking." This means that you are trying to treat a general truth like a mathematical certainty, which is not how proverbs were meant to be used.

The subtopic of testimonials can also be useful as you are constructing an argument. Testimonials are firsthand accounts of people's experiences. They are an informal type of authority, similar to proverbs. The experiences of regular people like you and me cover just about every imaginable situation, and therefore, the accounts, or testimonials, of those situations may provide valuable insight. The people giving these accounts may not be experts in these matters, but their experiences can still prove useful in an argument. For instance, a housewife who regularly uses a particular cleaning product might have valuable insight that would add credence to the cleaning product manufacturer's advertising campaign.

In your debate about uniforms, you might gather testimonials from students who wear school uniforms. Although these people are not experts, per se, their experiences might be enlightening. When you use testimonials to support your argument, you must realize that although testimonials can be helpful, they do not automatically prove a point, and they are usually not as powerful as evidence presented by authorities. In addition, you need to realize that people's individual memories, senses, and biases can distort their perception of a situation. For example, if five different people report on a situation, such as a car accident, they will usually report five very different versions of the same scenario. Furthermore, people sometimes lie about their experiences in an effort to receive fame, attention, or money. Therefore, you must consider testimonials with a healthy sense of skepticism.

Testimonials are firsthand accounts of people's experiences.

The use of the subtopic of Scripture can also be helpful in an argument. Christians regularly use the Bible as an authority in their discussions. However, because the Bible does not give direct commandments about every issue in life, it can sometimes be difficult to properly apply it as support for an argument. For instance, the Bible directly forbids stealing, killing, or lying, but it does not give specific commandments about fashion, music styles, playing golf, or watching TV. Nevertheless, people often cite the authority of the Bible on such issues. Because of this, Christians and others might wonder how to use this authority properly and how to determine whether or not others are using it properly. While an in-depth discussion of "**hermeneutics**," or the art and science of interpreting Scripture, is outside the scope of this book, there are a few general rules that can be applied to using Scripture in an argument and that will also apply to other types of authority.

When the Bible does not speak directly about a certain topic, most theologians (Bible experts) assert that we should then seek to determine if the Bible speaks indirectly about that topic by setting forth a general principle, which can then be applied to that topic. For instance, as mentioned above, while the Bible may not speak directly to modern fashion or overspending, it may speak to the importance of inner beauty and good financial stewardship (see 1 Peter 3:3-4 and Matthew 25:14-30). Modern questions about appropriate music and forms of recreation may be addressed by the biblical teachings about one's thought life and the stewardship of our talents and time, (see Philippians 4:8 and Ephesians 5:15-16). General biblical teachings about modesty (see 1 Timothy 2:9) and the wise use of money (see Matthew 25:14-30 and James 1:17) can be applied to modern concerns about dress and spending habits. When you use such biblical principles in an argument, it is helpful to look at all of Scripture—its stories, themes, and direct teachings—in order to be sure of the full biblical teaching of a particular principle. This can be challenging, so the use of a biblical concordance or topical Bible as resources can be helpful.

It is also important to see a biblical passage in context when you use it to prove a point. This means that you must use the verse in the way in which it was meant to be used, according to the chapter and verses surrounding it. A humorous story illustrates this point. A man who desired to know God's will said, "Lord, I am going to close my eyes. Then I am going to open my Bible, point to a verse on the page, and read it. I will know that whatever verse I point to will be your will." So the man did just that. When he opened his eyes, he was worried, for the verse read, "Judas...went away and hanged himself" (Matthew 27:5, NIV). Thinking that, perhaps, God was playing a little joke on him, the man tried it one more time. This time, when he opened his eyes, he read, "Go and do likewise" (Luke 10:37, NIV). This humorous story shows the folly of taking Bible verses out of context. By studying the context of these verses, one can quickly determine that we shouldn't emulate the character of Judas and that the "Go and do likewise" verse pertains to the story of the Good Samaritan, not suicide. You can see that taking a verse out of context can distort the true meaning of the passage. It is important, therefore, to determine just what subject a passage is addressing before you apply it to the subject of your liking.

You may have noticed that the rules for using arguments from authorities, proverbs, testimonials, and Scripture all follow a certain pattern. When you use these argument techniques, you need to make sure that you understand them in the context of the argument. You must apply the words of an authority to the situations in which they were intended to be used. In addition, in the case of human authorities or testimonials, don't automatically accept a claim because a person is an expert or because she has had a relevant experience. Authorities and people who give testimonials can make mistakes or be purposely deceptive. Lastly, since the Bible is a sacred book, you should show extra care so as not to misrepresent it as source in an argument.

DEFINE

1. Authorities: ______

2. Proverbs: ______

3. Clichéd Thinking: ______

4. Direct Biblical Instruction: ______

5. Indirect Biblical Instruction: ______

WRITE

Write a brief paragraph that explains several general principles you should follow when using arguments from authority.

General Rules for Arguments from Authorities

______

ANSWER

Examples of Arguments from Authority: Read each of the provided examples and then answer the questions following each of the excerpts.

1. In this excerpt from **The Friendship Factor,** *author Alan Loy McGinnis describes the importance of friendship.*

Jesus placed great value on relationships. He chose to spend much of his time deepening his connections with a few significant persons rather than addressing the crowds. What is more, his teaching was filled with practical suggestions on how to befriend people and how to relate to friends. The commandment on this topic was so important that he introduced it with an opening flag: "A new commandment I give to you, that you love one another; even as I have loved you, that you also love one another. By this all men will know that you are my disciples, if you have love for one another" (John 13:34-35).

Those words are now almost 2000 years old, but their currency is demonstrated in a recent study. In his book *The Broken Heart*, Dr. James J. Lynch shows that lonely people live significantly shorter lives than the general population. Lynch, who is a specialist in psychosomatic disease, cites a wealth of statistics to demonstrate the unhealthy aspects of isolation and the magical powers of human contact.[1]

a. State McGinnis' thesis in your own words. ____________________

b. What two authorities does McGinnis use to support his thesis? Are these authorities both legitimate? Support your answer.

c. Is McGinnis' use of Scripture appropriate? Support your answer.

ANSWER

2. Francis Bacon's "Of Revenge"

Certainly, in taking revenge, a man is but even with his enemy; but in passing it over, he is superior; for it is a prince's part to pardon. And Solomon, I am sure, saith, "It is the glory of a man, to pass by an offence."[2]

a. What person does Bacon quote from in support of his idea about revenge? ________________

b. Is the quoted person's statement used more as an authority or as a maxim or proverb? How do you know? ________________

c. Is Bacon's use of this person's words appropriate, considering the rules for using authorities and proverbs? Explain your answer. ________________

ANSWER

3. This excerpt from **Primal Leadership** *discusses the way in which powerful emotions can affect those who come in contact with them.*

Emotions may spread like viruses, but not all emotions spread with the same ease. A study at the Yale University School of Management found that among working groups, cheerfulness and warmth spread most easily, while irritability is less contagious and depression spreads hardly at all.[3]

a. Who is the authority in this excerpt? ________________

b. What two things make the authority referenced in this excerpt especially legitimate for the claim being made? ________________

Dress Code and Arguments from Authority

1. In the Research exercise in chapter 6, you used library and Internet resources to find information about school uniforms. Choose several of those sources you gathered for that exercise and skim the information to find the author's main idea and the evidence he uses to support his conclusions. Is the author for or against school uniforms? What evidence does he use to support his theories? Does he have credible expertise in this area?

2. Find a quote book at your local library or in your classroom. What quotes can you find that are associated with dress code or related subjects? Remember, proverbs and quotes are only general ideas, not ironclad formulas, so be careful that you don't use them this way.

3. What stories, principles, and verses can you find in Scripture that seem to relate to dress code? The Bible does not speak directly about dress code, so, once again, you will want to search for ideas related to the topics we mentioned above and apply them generally to dress code. Remember to consider what the whole of Scripture says about these issues and to take the passages in context.

BRAINSTORM

Now that you understand how to use arguments from authority, use this subtopic to brainstorm some arguments from authority for the uniform debate. Use the provided questions to help you, and then write a paragraph that has both a topic and concluding sentence about uniforms. The paragraph should explain at least three types of support from authorities, proverbs, or the Bible. Be aware that you may not be able to find any information directly about school uniforms (but you may). If you can't, then find information pertaining to dress, order, discipline, clothing, or other topics related to uniforms, and use the ideas that seem to apply generally to uniforms.

CHAPTER 8 *Fallacies of Testimony*

Now that we have examined the different subtopics of testimony—examples, statistics, authority, proverbs, and Scripture—let's look at some common fallacies that people make with this common topic.

The common topic of testimony often requires you to consult books or other written sources to find examples, proverbs or ideas from various authorities. Whenever you consult written sources, there is a greater chance that you will commit a factual or copying error. Therefore, make sure that you accurately record ideas from the sources you consult.

The first fallacy associated with this common topic, accent, is closely related to an error of fact. Sometimes when a person reports someone's words, he reports the words correctly, but he leaves out key ideas and distorts the meaning of the words. For instance, you might se a movie review that looks something like this: "This movie is a brilliant…work…. You will have the time of your life!" This looks like a great review, but if you read the critic's original comments, he actually said something like this: "This movie is a brilliantly idiotic piece of work, and you will have the time of your life if you enjoy dying a slow, painful and stupid death in a movie theatre!" The first quote contained the actual words of the reviewer, but it was edited in a way that totally distorted the original idea. This illustrates the fallacy of accent. When someone commits this fallacy, she only reports part of an event or part of someone's words, and the effect is distortion and error.

A second fallacy people commit with the common topic of testimony is clichéd thinking. When someone commits the fallacy of clichéd thinking, most likely when using a proverb or famous saying, he applies a general principle as though it is an ironclad rule. For example, most of us are familiar with the common saying, "The early bird catches the worm." This principle generally indicates that people who get up early and get to work right away will be more prosperous than those who sleep in all the time and are late getting to work. However, a person would commit the fallacy of clichéd thinking if he applied this saying to his life in this way: "I get up at 5 o'clock every morning and go straight to work. Therefore, I will certainly be wealthy and prosperous." This is a fallacy because this person is mistakenly attempting to apply a general principle as a mathematical formula. General principles, such as those found in quote books by famous people, or even in the book of Proverbs, are meant to be illustrations of the way life usually works. The proverbs do not come with a 100 percent guarantee.

In other words, proverbs and wise sayings are not meant to be interpreted as a picture of the way life works 100 percent of the time. As another example, consider that Proverbs states that we will be happy if we gain understanding and knowledge (see Proverbs 3:13, NKJV). However, you probably know some very wise and knowledgeable people who are sad and maybe even miserable. Of course, this doesn't prove that Proverbs 3:13 is wrong or that it "doesn't work." It is usually true that gaining wisdom and knowledge leads to greater happiness. However, even really wise people

have bad days. The point is that when you use wise sayings or proverbs in your arguments, make sure you use them as just that: wise saying from which we can gain general knowledge about life. Don't use them as ironclad formulas or mathematical principles or you will be committing the fallacy of clichéd thinking.

The next fallacy, the bandwagon fallacy, is another error people commit when they use the common topic of testimony incorrectly. You might remember that in the first chapter, we mentioned the "But all of my friends…" appeal to your mother and father concerning curfew. As I noted, when children use this argument, parents automatically reply, "If all of your friends jumped off a bridge, would you do it, too?" The flaw of the "All of my friends are doing it" argument is that groups of people have been known to believe and do stupid and dangerous things. Therefore, even if everyone *is* doing or thinking something, it doesn't mean that it is right. For example, only a few decades ago, smoking was considered a socially popular thing to do, and many people even believed it was good for their health. Today we realize that this is incorrect. When we use testimonials and appeals to authority, it is important to remember that mass opinion can be wrong. Therefore, we need to examine the merit of each argument, rather than placing blind trust in "the group."

The next fallacy that occurs with the use of the common topic of testimony is hasty generalization. Remember that when we use inductive logic, we base a general principle on several examples. When someone commits hasty generalization, she bases a generalization on an atypical or anomalous example. For instance, we have all heard examples of people who fall from really high buildings and, miraculously, live to tell about it. If you decide, after witnessing one such occurrence, that jumping off high buildings is a safe pastime, you are making a hasty generalization. Most people who jump from or fall off high buildings die or sustain terrible injuries. The people who survive are anomalies, offering an atypical example of what happens when you fall from a great height, and you do not want to make a generalization from their experience. The principle demonstrated by this fallacy can also be applied to statistics. Remember that most good statistical studies are based on a large, randomly selected sample. The larger the sample size, the less likely we are to encounter anomalies, such as the girls' volleyball team in the "purple is dangerous" argument, that distort the statistic.

The last fallacy that applies to the common topic of testimony is illegitimate appeal to authority. When someone commits this fallacy, he uses the expertise of an authority to support a thesis outside of that authority's field of expertise. As I mentioned before, commercials frequently contain this fallacy. For instance, advertisers use movie stars to sell a variety of things from cola to cars. These people often have no expertise in the matters they are advertising, but the advertisers are hoping the public will buy the products because of the movie stars' good looks, popularity and "coolness." Similarly, if you are not careful, you might use people's expertise incorrectly in an effort to dazzle others, and this may take away from the validity of your argument. Keep in mind that when someone commits illegitimate appeal to authority, the authority to which he is referring does have *some* type of expertise, it's just not the right kind of expertise to support the person's argument.

As you learn more about fallacies, remember that logic dictates that you consider every argument to determine the conclusion of the argument and the evidence supporting the conclusion. If you do this throughout your day, you will be surprised at how many seemingly logical arguments actually contain the fallacies we are studying. Continue to review the common topics and fallacies we have studied so far, and you will grow in your ability to practice good logic.

DEFINE

1. Accent: ______________________________

2. Bandwagon: ______________________________

3. Hasty Generalization: ______________________________

4. Illegitimate Appeal to Authority: ______________________________

REVIEW

So far, you have studied the common topics of definition and testimony. Take a few minutes to review these common topics and their subtopics and then answer the provided questions.

The Common Topics

1. What two things must you define before you begin a proper argument?

2. Why is defining these two things important? ______________________________

3. List four definition techniques:

4. List three subtopics under the common topic of testimony:

ANALYZE

Fallacy Alert: Read each of the arguments. Explain what fallacy is being committed in each and then explain why the premises do not support the conclusion.

1. I have decided I am going to buy a Toyota for my next car. I saw a commercial in which my favorite golfer was advocating the brand, and I really admire his golfing skills!

2. I will never go to Taco Heaven again. One time I went, and there was a robbery that night. Taco Heaven is a dangerous place!

3. A teenager says to her parents, "You have to get me a car for graduation. Every single other person in my class is getting one for graduation!"

4. A newspaper published a supposedly favorable review of a book for a local author. The review read as follows: "This book is an amazing example of sheer…literature. You will never want to…read another book…again."

5. You've got to go to Florida on spring break. Everyone is going there!

6. Doctor Phillips, noted professor of archaeology, has thoroughly endorsed the new neighborhood safety plan. Therefore, we can adopt it with confidence!

CHAPTER 9 *Review of Definitions and Testimony*

You have studied the common topics of definition and testimony, and you have considered how to use these common topics to develop arguments about curfew and uniforms. The following essay uses the common topics of definition and testimony to develop a more abstract concept than what you have studied so far. Read the following essay and then complete the review exercises that follow.

The Two Sides of Justice

It is common to read about groups or individuals who believe that their rights have been violated and who demand justice. Justice is a concept that the Greek philosopher Plato valued greatly and a concept frequently addressed in the Bible. In addition, it is one of those "inalienable rights" of which our forefathers spoke in the Declaration of Independence. In the declaration, Thomas Jefferson wrote, "We hold these truths to be self-evident, that all men are created equal, that they are endowed by their Creator with certain unalienable rights, that among these are life, liberty and the pursuit of happiness."[1] These are certainly words of justice.

In order to understand the true meaning of justice, we must consider its origins. The word "justice" derives from the Latin word *justus*, which carries the idea of "straight or close; setting, extending, erecting; regular, orderly, due, sensible; exactly proportional."[2] It is important to remember that the idea of making things exactly proportional or giving a person his due is integral to the concept of justice. People often only think of justice in a positive sense, but it also has a negative sense. In the positive sense, justice gives people valuable commodities, such as rights, property, and opportunity in order to make situations more equal or fair. In its negative sense, justice restores things to their rightful owner, removes unfair advantages, and metes out punishment.

Although justice contains both of these concepts, most people demand negative justice for others and desire mercy or unjust privilege for themselves. For instance, in Shakespeare's *Merchant of Venice*, Shylock pursues unmitigated justice for his enemy, Antonio, which will cause Antonio's death. Yet when the judge informs Shylock that if Antonio receives unmitigated justice, so must Shylock, Shylock immediately relinquishes his demands for pure justice. This is often the way we humans approach justice. When justice hurts our enemy, we are its strongest advocate, but we do not desire justice when it hurts us. As Daniel Defoe once said, "Justice is always violent to the party offending, for every man is innocent in his own eyes."[3] H.L. Menken noted with insight that "Injustice is relatively easy to bear; what stings is justice."[4]

Justice is both beautiful and terrible. So what, then, shall we do with justice? Shall we abandon its pursuit because it often brings pain as well as relief? No. As Martin Luther King once said, "Injustice anywhere is a threat to justice everywhere."[5] To neglect justice when one sees its need is to participate in a host of evils. We must always recognize injustice and address it. That often requires punishment, yet it also requires humility, mercy, sacrifice, and forgiveness.

—Shelly Johnson

ANSWER

1. State the thesis of this essay in your own words. ______________________________

2. List two definition techniques that are used in this essay. ______________________________

3. List two authorities that are used in this essay. ______________________________

4. List two other techniques used in this essay to develop the thesis. ______________________________

PRACTICE

This essay developed a thesis about an abstract concept using several common topics. Choose a similar concept and use the common topics that you have learned about so far to develop a thesis for the topic. The following are some possible topics you could choose: love, hate, mercy, wisdom, ignorance, cruelty, generosity, faithfulness, cowardice, truthfulness, dishonesty. (You may also choose your own topic). When you have chosen your topic, write a thesis statement. Then use at least three definition techniques and three types of testimony to develop your thesis statement. Organize all of this information into several well-structured paragraphs.

Common Topic 3

Comparison

Imagine the beginning of a new school year. You are excited about seeing all of your friends and a little nervous about meeting your new teachers. Some of these teachers may have taught you in the past, but you will also have new teachers. You are anxious to understand these new teachers so that you can do well in class. In order to do this, you might have observed your new teachers and reasoned in this way: "This new teacher reminds me a lot of Mrs. Nemen. Mrs. Nemen got annoyed when we talked during instructions. I need to remember to pay attention to this teacher and not sit by people who distract me." Or you might think, "This teacher is very tough just like Mr. Langley, my English teacher from last semester. I never knew whether he was going to test out of the book or from the notes. I think I am going to make really good outlines from the class and my book and find a study partner to make sure I know the information thoroughly."

Later you might discover that your comparisons were partially correct but partially incorrect. For instance, you may discover as your class progresses that the teacher who reminded you of Mr. Langley is tough, but he primarily tests from his lectures, so you readjust your study habits based on this difference. When you reason in this way, you are using the common topic of comparison. There are several subtopics of comparison that allow us to compare two things in other ways when are studying a new subject. Let's look at each of the possible comparisons we could use as well as some fallacies that occur within the common topic of comparison.

Analogy: This subtopic supports a conclusion by examining the similarities between two examples. When constructing arguments from analogies, it important to avoid the fallacy of **false analogy**. A false analogy draws a conclusion from a comparison of two examples that are far too dissimilar to warrant any logical conclusion.

Difference: This argument strategy forms a conclusion by examining the dissimilarities between two examples.

Degree: This type of argument supports a conclusion by examining how two examples relate to one another on scales of worth, possibility, value, or other such measurements. ***A fortiori*** arguments (literally "from the stronger") are a type of argument from degree that specifically explores whether or not something is likely to exist. There are two types of *a fortiori* arguments: arguments from the greater to the lesser or from the lesser to the greater.

As we explore each of these subtopics of comparison, remember that you will use examples to develop them, just as you will with many of the common topics.

CHAPTER 10 *Subtopic: Analogy*

One of the most effective types of arguments, an analogy compares two examples in order to draw a conclusion based on relevant similarities between the two examples. Analogies can be illuminating because they often compare abstract concepts to more familiar concepts. For example, in the New Testament Jesus often used analogies to explain abstract concepts, such as when He compared the kingdom of heaven to a mustard seed (see Matthew 13:31-32), and his followers to the lilies of the field that do not worry about clothing and yet are beautifully clothed by God (see Matthew 6:28-30).

Analogies can be an effective tool for constructing good arguments. For instance, suppose a person is arguing about the Civil War and this is his thesis statement: "It was unjust for the South to secede from the North." To support his thesis statement, this person might compare the Union of the North and South to a marriage: "In a marriage, two people should not divorce when they face trouble. Instead, they should stay together and work through the problems. In the same way, the South should have stayed with the North and worked through their disagreements."

On the other hand, let's say a person was arguing the opposite thesis: "It was just for the South to secede from the North." She might use the following analogy: "It was perfectly just for the South to secede from the North because the Union was like a contract. When two parties make a contract, each party promises to fulfill certain duties and obligations. If one party fails to fulfill its duties or obligations, the other party is released from the contract. Before the Civil War, the North failed to fulfill its promises and duties, so the South was released from its contract." Using common examples like a marriage and a union can clarify a difficult subject such as secession. Of course, in order to use these analogies appropriately, each person should support the analogy with other evidence, such as historical examples and quotes from authority.

You will notice that both of the preceding analogies were developed in a similar pattern. First, the person stated the two items being compared. For example, in the first analogy, the person compared the Union to a marriage. Then the person explained the first part of the analogy. In the example above, the person explained that two married people should work through difficulties rather than seek divorce. Finally, the person explained how the second part of the analogy was similar to the first. For example, the arguer explained that the South should have worked through its difficulties with the North instead of seceding from the Union. If you find it difficult to form analogies, this is a good pattern to follow as you are learning the process.

Think about how you could use the subtopic of analogies with your curfew debate. First of all, you want two examples similar to curfew. Here are some possibilities:

Curfew is like a fence around a playground.

Curfew is like a traffic signal.

Curfew is like a safety rail at the edge of a mountain.

As you might have noticed, most of these possible comparisons follow a pattern. We are comparing curfew to other boundaries that provide direction or protection. When you are searching for an appropriate analogy, you will likely find several possible comparisons. If this happens, choose the example that parallels the most important points of your topic. For example, as you discuss curfew with your parents, you want to convince them to establish a curfew that is a flexible guide, rather than a rigid rule. Because of this, it might be good to use the first analogy mentioned above: Curfew is like a fence around a playground. Fences are flexible boundaries that can be reconfigured to better accomplish their purpose. It would not be as effective to compare curfew to a traffic signal because traffic signals are part of a uniform, rigid system that is not usually adapted to different situations. Therefore, the fence example has more relevant similarities to curfew than the traffic signal example.

To develop this analogy, you should explain the similarities between a curfew and a playground fence. You might word the analogy like this: "Curfews are like fences around playgrounds. People put a fence around playground so that kids can roam freely and play in the playground while still being protected from dangers outside the fence. The people who put up the fence can arrange the fence any way they choose as long as they allow the children freedom while still protecting them from danger. In the same way, curfew rules allow young adults some freedom and responsibility while still protecting them from dangers. Just as with a fence, there are a number of ways a curfew can be established, as long as it allows the young adults some freedom and protects them from danger." This analogy is strong because it demonstrates that fences can be moved and rearranged to suit different needs, and this flexibility is also what you want with your curfew. Remember that you can usually develop an analogy in several different ways. The key is to emphasize the similarities that best support your thesis statement.

As you search for analogies to support your thesis statement, look for common, well-known examples that contain similarities relevant to your topic. You will always be able to find a number of similar examples, but some examples will not be as relevant as others. When you find a good example for comparison, it will support your thesis statement by illuminating some confusing or controversial part of your topic.

Analogies can be illuminating because they often compare abstract concepts to more familiar concepts.

ANSWER

1. Describe what an analogy is and how it works. ______________________________
____
____
____

2. If you discover many possible examples for a comparison to your topic, how can you choose the best example to use in an analogy? ______________________________
____
____
____

3. When you were examining possible examples to compare to a curfew, one of the examples was a safety rail at the edge of a mountain road. Would this be a good example to use in a curfew analogy? Why or why not? ______________________________
____
____
____

SELECT

Good Examples for Comparison: Each provided item contains a phrase that is the beginning of an analogy. Read the phrase and then circle the example that best completes the analogy. Be prepared to explain why you chose the example you did.

1. Too much sun can cause skin cancer just like
   a. Too much homework can make you tired.
   b. Spending too much money can make you poor.
   c. Pouring too much milk can cause a glass to overflow.
   d. Eating too much candy can make you sick.
2. Students must do activities to strengthen their brains just like
   a. People need to work in their houses to make them clean.
   b. People need to exercise their muscles to improve endurance.
   c. People must earn money in order to buy Christmas presents.
   d. People must brush their teeth in order to make them clean.
3. People experience the consequences of their actions just like
   a. A person robs a bank to steal money.
   b. A farmer reaps the crops he sows.
   c. A twin brother and sister look alike.
   d. A painter gets money for selling his painting.
4. A teacher must coax her students to strive for excellence like
   a. A circus trainer must whip a lion to make it move.
   b. A drill sergeant must shout and scream to motivate his troops.
   c. A dynamite engineer must light a fuse to cause an explosion.
   d. An orchestra conductor must direct his orchestra to bring forth beautiful music

IDENTIFY

Famous Analogies: Each of the provided excerpts contains an analogy. For each excerpt, identify the thesis statement and the two examples being compared in the analogy. Because these paragraphs were written many centuries ago, the language will be a little unusual. Take your time to read and reread them to determine their meanings.

1. From Francis Bacon's "Of Unity in Religion"

We shall therefore speak a few words, concerning the unity of the church; what are the fruits thereof; what the bounds; and what the means. The fruits of unity…are two: the one, towards those that are without the church, the other towards those that are within. For the former, it is certain that heresies, and schisms, are of all others the grandest scandals; yea, more than corruption of manner. For as in the natural body, a wound or solution of continuity, is worse than a corrupt humor, so in the spiritual. So that nothing, doth so much keep men out of the church and drive men out of the church as breach of unity.[1]

Thesis Statement: ____

____

____

____

Two Examples: ____

____

____

____

IDENTIFY

2. From Augustine's "On Christian Doctrine"

In what way did He come but this, "The Word was made flesh, and dwelt among us"? Just as when we speak, in order that what we have in our minds may enter through the ear into the mind of the hearer, the word which we have in our hearts becomes an outward sound and is called speech; and yet our thought does not lose itself in the sound, but remains complete in itself, and takes the form of speech without being modified in its own nature by the change: so the Divine Word, though suffering no change of nature, yet became flesh, that He might dwell in us.[2]

Thesis Statement: ____

____

____

____

Two Examples: ____

____

____

____

IDENTIFY

3. From Augustine's **On Christian Doctrine**

Suppose, then, we were wanderers in a strange country, and could not live happily away from our fatherland, and that we felt wretched in our wandering, and wishing to put an end to our misery, determined to return home. We find, however, that we must make use of some mode of conveyance, either by land or water, in order to reach that fatherland where our enjoyment is to commence. But the beauty of the country through which we pass, and the very pleasure of the motion, charm our hearts, and turning these things which we ought to use into objects of enjoyment, we become unwilling to hasten the end of our journey; and becoming engrossed in a factitious delight, our thoughts are diverted from that home whose delights would make us truly happy. Such is a picture of our condition in this life of mortality. We have wandered far from God; and if we wish to return to our Father's home, this world must be used, not enjoyed, that so the invisible things of God may be clearly seen, being understood by the things that are made—that is, that by means of what is material and temporary we may lay hold upon that which is spiritual and eternal.[3]

Thesis Statement: ______________________________

____

____

____

Two Examples: ______________________________

____

____

CONSIDER

Uniforms and Arguments from Analogy: Consider how you could develop an analogy to support your uniform thesis statement. For this exercise, you may use the thesis statement for uniforms that I provided, or you may use the one that you have already thought up and tailor the exercise accordingly. For this exercise, we will define uniforms as khaki or navy blue pants or skirts and a white, blue or red collared oxford shirt that the students must wear every day to school.

Thesis statement: School uniforms establish an ordered school environment.

Using this or your own thesis statement as your guide, think of one comparison that supports the thesis statement and one comparison that counters this statement. I have provided two example possibilities below.

Uniforms are like fences that form boundaries around playgrounds.

Uniforms are like straightjackets.

Supports: Uniforms are like ______________________________

____

____

____

____

Counters: Uniforms are like ______________________________

____

____

____

____

CRAFT

Alternate Analogies: Choose one of the thesis statements from the previous exercises. Then craft a new analogy that proves this same thesis. Write a short paragraph that contains the thesis statement and the fully developed new analogy.

WRITE

Analogy Paragraphs: Choose one of the analogies you came up with in the previous exercise and write a paragraph that fully explains the analogy.

The following is a good formula to follow for developing your paragraph:

1. Write a topic sentence that contains your thesis statement.
2. Briefly explain why your topic is important.
3. Give an analogy beginning with a phrase such as, "It is like…."
4. Show how the two parts of the analogy are similar using a phrase such as, "In the same way…."
5. Give a concluding motivational thought or call to action.

CHAPTER 11 *Subtopic: Differences*

When you were little, did your mom or dad ever say, "Don't be a tattletale"? If you have brothers or sisters, your parents probably said this to you regularly. After you were scolded several times for being a tattletale, you probably realized that it was wrong to tattle about annoying but essentially harmless actions. You may have also realized it was wrong to tattle about a misdeed for the sheer joy of getting your siblings in trouble, such as when your brother ate ten fresh chocolate chip cookies, and you tattled immediately, hoping he would get the spanking of his life (it's OK, you can admit it; we've all done it). After a few tries of similar behavior at school, with subsequent scoldings from your teacher, you most likely realized that tattling was wrong at school as well as at home. To refer to what you learned in chapter 10, you used an *analogy* to generalize that adults disapprove of tattling.

Now imagine a new scenario. You are in junior high, and you become aware that one of your classmates is cheating regularly on tests. You also discover that several bullies are harassing a fellow classmate at lunchtime. The cheating and bullying bother you, and you want to tell an authority figure. At first, however, when you consider this, you immediately hear an internal voice scolding, "Don't be a tattletale." However, as you considered the situation, you realize that these incidents are different from those in your childhood because cheating and bullying are very different from petty sibling rivalries. The more you consider the situation, the more you realize that if someone doesn't stop the cheating and the bullying, these situations could become more serious. In addition, as you examine your motives, you realize that you desire to report these misdemeanors so that justice is done, not so that people will suffer. You eventually decide that telling someone about these situations is, in fact, the honorable thing to do, rather than being dishonorable and petty as tattling about a less important situation might be.

In order to reach this conclusion, you made a comparison between your current situation and situations in your childhood. However, rather than basing your conclusion on the *similarities* of the two situations, as you would when using the subtopic of analogy, you based your conclusion on the *differences* between them. In other words, you used the argument of difference, which is the second subtopic of the common topic of comparison. When you use the subtopic of difference, you form premises by examining the dissimilarities of examples. You have probably used this argument technique in school without even realizing it. For example, in history class, you may have contrasted two rulers to determine which of their leadership styles was most effective, or you may have compared two wars to determine which one was more just or more influential in a country's history. In literature, you have probably examined two characters who were completely different from one another in order to better understand the personality of one or both characters. As these examples imply, it can be helpful in understanding an example by studying another example that is different from it.

Let's look at your argument about curfew using this subtopic. A curfew is similar to other rules your parents gave you as you were growing up, such as, "Don't put your hand on the stove burner," or "Don't cross the street before looking both ways." However, curfew rules are different from these other rules because curfew governs the lives of young adults who are gaining responsibility but who still need some guidelines to help them use that responsibility wisely. This is an important distinction to make because, while the first set of rules are more or less non-negotiable (you never reach an age when it's wise to put your hand on a hot burner), curfew rules are the kind of rules that are more flexible and can change to adapt to different situations. If you can develop this difference into an argument, it will help your debate.

You may have noticed that using the subtopic of difference requires you to use the definition technique of genus and species, which we discussed in an earlier chapter. When you use the common topic of comparison, you compare two examples in a genus, and you form a conclusion from their similarities or differences. As I have mentioned several times, and as you will continue to see as you study the common topics further, you will often use the techniques of one common topic to help develop another common topic.

ANSWER

1. What are some comparisons and contrasts between the subtopics of analogy and difference?

EXAMINE

Arguments from Difference: Read each of the provided excerpts. Determine the two things that are being contrasted and explain the difference mentioned in the excerpt.

1. From Montaigne's "Of Fear"

The thing in the world I am most afraid of is fear, that passion alone, in the trouble of it, exceeding all other accidents. What affliction could be greater or more just than that of Pompey's friends, who, in this ship were spectators of that horrible murder? Yet so it was, that the fear of the Egyptian vessels they saw coming to board them, possess them with so great alarm that it is observed they thought of nothing but calling upon the mariners to make haste, and by force of oars to escape away, till being arrived at Tyre, and delivered from fear, they had leisure to turn their thoughts to the loss of their captain, and to give vent to those tears and lamentations that the other more potent passions had till then suspended.... The Greeks acknowledge another kind of fear, differing from any we have spoken of yet, that surprises us without any visible cause, by an impulse from heaven, so that whole nations and whole armies have been struck with it. Such a one was that which brought so wonderful a desolation upon Carthage, where nothing was to be heard but affrighted voices and outcries; where the inhabitants were seen to sally out of their houses as to an alarm, and there to charge, wound, and kill one another, as if they had been enemies come to surprise their city. All things were in disorder and fury till, with prayers and sacrifices, they had appeased their gods; and this is that. They call a panic terror.[1]

EXAMINE

2. From John Ruskin's "Taste in Literature"

I know many persons who have the purest taste in literature, and yet false taste in art, and it is a phenomenon which puzzles me not a little; but I have never known anyone with false taste in books, and true taste in pictures. It is also of the greatest importance to you, not only for art's sake, but for all kinds of sake, in these days of book deluge, to keep out of the salt swamps of literature, and live on a little rocky island of your own with a spring and a lake in it, pure and good. I cannot, of course, suggest the choice of your library to you, every several mind needs different books; but there are some books which we all need, and assuredly, you read Homer, Plato Aeschylus, Herodotus, Dante, Shakespeare, and Spencer, as much as you ought, you will not require wide enlargement of shelves to the right and left of them for purposes of perpetual study. Among modern books, avoid generally magazine and review literature. Sometimes it may contain a useful abridgment or a wholesome piece of criticism; but the chances are ten to one it will either waste your time or mislead you.[2]

DEVELOP

Using Arguments from Difference: Use the subtopic of difference to develop your arguments for your thesis on uniforms. This can be a tricky subtopic to use for generating arguments because while you may be able to think of several examples that are different from your topic, how do you know what kinds of differences are pertinent? To help you discover these pertinent differences, consider the provided questions.

1. If you are arguing *for* the adoption of school uniforms, consider some negative examples that your opponent might compare to uniforms. How can you show that uniforms are different from this negative example and that they can be a positive influence in a school?

DEVELOP

2. If you are arguing *against* the adoption of school uniforms, what are some positive examples your opponent might compare to uniforms? How can you show that uniforms are different from this positive example and can bring negative consequences in a school atmosphere?

3. Proponents of school uniforms often believe that adopting a school uniform will have positive results, such as increased discipline, order, and productivity. If you are arguing *against* uniforms, how can you demonstrate that different and potentially negative results are likely to ensue with the adoption of school uniforms (e.g., mounting frustration, decrease of personal expression)? Opponents of uniforms often believe that abolishing school uniforms will have positive results on students, such as improving student comfort, decreasing teacher-student conflicts, and providing more opportunity for students' personal expression. If you are arguing *for* school uniforms, how can you demonstrate that different, and potentially negative, results are likely to ensue with the abolition of school uniforms (e.g., sloppiness, disrespect, immodesty, and distractions)?

CHAPTER 12 *Subtopic: Degree*

Can you remember a time when you had to choose between several good options? For instance, you decided to watch a movie Friday night, and you had to choose between six new releases, all of which seemed appealing. How did you determine which one to watch? Perhaps you were in the mood for a comedy that night, and so you picked the most humorous one. On the other hand, maybe the last movie you watched was a comedy, so you chose the most dramatic movie instead.

Let's consider an opposite scenario. Can you remember a time when you had to choose between several *bad* options? Perhaps you needed to take some cold medicine, but all of them had negative side effects. One would make you sleepy, the other would make you feel a little dizzy, and the third one had a horrible aftertaste. In this case, you had to pick which one was the least problematic for your current situation. For instance, if you were taking the medicine at the beginning of the day before school, you might choose one that would not make you sleepy so that you could stay awake during classes.

When students go to college, they often use the subtopic of degree to choose classes. For instance, many college students must take required classes that they don't necessarily like. However, they may discover that there are several different sections of the class, which are taught at different times of the day by different teachers. Although the students may not like the particular class, they can choose a section taught at a better time of day or by a more energetic teacher. When students make decisions like this, they are using the subtopic of degree. The subtopic of degree often helps you to determine the relative worth of an example or choice. For instance, it may help you decide if a choice or example is better or worse, stronger or weaker, more or less likely, or of greater or lesser virtue. These are only a few types of relative worth that you might consider when using the subtopic of degree. The following are some other examples of relative worth that you can use with this subtopic:

1. *A greater number of things can be considered more desirable than a smaller number of the same things.*[1] For example, people tend to value farming methods that produce more food rather than less food. People who earn more money through their stock market investments are considered more successful than those who earn less money.

2. *That which is an end is a greater good than that which is only considered a means.*[2] Usually the end product of a process is greater or more valuable than those tools or methods that help achieve the end. For example, you study hard in order to gain a good education. You exercise heartily to improve your health. Though you value study and exercise, you value their end product more.

3. *What is scarce is greater than what is abundant.*[3] When items are scarce, they are more valuable. Therefore, precious jewels, gold, unpolluted water, and good friends are all valuable because of their scarcity.

4. *What a person who has practical wisdom would choose is a greater good than what an ignorant person would choose.*[4] We consult authorities for this very reason. We assume that the advice of a wiser, better-educated person is greater than that of a less-educated person.

5. *What the minority of people would choose is better than what the majority of people would choose.*[5] Doctors and health professionals recommend that to achieve good health people should get thirty minutes of some type of physical exercise at least three times a week. Only a small minority of people in the United States actually achieve this recommended goal. Many health professionals believe that this is because Americans are too busy and that, unfortunately, many people don't truly value the health benefits of physical exercise. Therefore, the people who do get the recommended amount of physical exercise could be more disciplined or well informed than those who do not. This example illustrates the statement that minority groups often know better than the majority does.

6. *If a thing does not exist where it is more likely to exist, it will not exist where it is less likely to exist.*[6] For example, imagine that a boy named Paul gets a new bike and wants to go on a seven-mile bike ride with his father. Paul's father is not sure if Paul can handle riding that distance. However, that weekend, Paul visits a friend who has a ten-mile bike path near his house. When Paul returns home, he informs his dad that he rode the entire ten-mile path and wasn't tired at all. Paul's father will likely reason that because his son did not get tired on the ten-mile ride (which was more likely), he will not tire out on the seven-mile ride (which is less likely).

The last argument that we examined above is a special type of argument called an *a fortiori* argument, which can be very helpful in a debate.[7] In Latin, *a fortiori* literally means "from the stronger." The Bible uses a lot of *a fortiori* arguments. For example, in the Sermon on the Mount, Jesus said that we should not worry because if God provides clothes for the lilies of the field, God will certainly provide clothes for us because we are more important than the lilies (see Matthew 6:28-30). This is an *a fortiori* argument because Jesus demonstrated that if God provides for less important things, such as lilies of the field, he will care for more important things, such as human beings. When you use an *a fortiori a*rgument, you can argue from the weaker to the stronger, as in the biblical argument about the lilies of the field, or you can argue from the stronger to the weaker, as in the example about Paul and his bike ride.

Let's consider some degree arguments that might work for your curfew discussion. First of all, it is important to admit that many of your parents' rules are good. After all, they care about you and want to protect you. So, it is important that you admit that their curfew rule is not completely inappropriate. However, it may be that there is a greater good they should consider. For instance, your safety is certainly a good goal, but a greater goal may be the development of your personal sense of responsibility. Therefore, you might argue that, while you understand the necessity of curfews, you believe that a curfew that allows experience in responsibility is better than one that only focuses on personal safety.

A similar, but slightly different, argument from degree may also be effective here. As you remember, one of the possible arguments from degree is "that which is an end is a greater good than that which is only considered a means." In the case of your curfew, your parents' end goal is that you be a responsible, autonomous adult. Protecting you is a means to the end of your reaching adulthood safely. Most parents would agree that at some point they must allow their children greater and greater freedom so the children can face the real world, even if it means the children might encounter some danger. Perhaps you can argue with your parents that when you are an adult, you will be in situations in which you must drive late at night, even in bad weather. Therefore, your proposed curfew will help you accomplish an important end goal: appropriately handling difficult situations, such as driving at night in bad weather.

The subtopic of degree can also be a helpful argument technique because it can aid in the clarity of your argument. When you are arguing with someone, it is wise to recognize any common ground between your stance and your opponent's. In other words, if you can agree with your opponent about something, do so, and then discuss the points of disagreement that remain. This not only creates an atmosphere of civility, it also clarifies the most important points under discussion.

For example, in the United States, many people disagree about how we should help poverty-stricken Americans. I think most people agree that helping poor people who are the victims of injustice and tragedy is the right thing to do, but that encouraging dependence on the government is detrimental to people's work ethic and character. In addition, most people would agree that the best way for people to escape poverty is to learn to provide for themselves, and that giving money to capable people who refuse to work is unwise. If people recognized these common beliefs, it might help them focus on a discussion of the methods that would be the most successful in helping people accomplish the goals of financial independence and prosperity. Unfortunately, when people, particularly those in the political arena, discuss this issue, they spend a great deal of time disparaging each other's motives and character rather than discussing the best means for achieving shared goals. Of course, there are times when people share very few, if any, beliefs. If that is the case, you should not manufacture points of agreement, but you can still be civil in your disagreement.

The subtopic of degree can help you discover the most effective means for accomplishing shared goals, which is an effective process in any argument. Someone once said that the mark of an educated person is that he or she can entertain an idea without accepting it. This is certainly the mark of a logical, reasonable person, as well. As you begin to mature in your logic skills, you will find that you are able to consider your opponent's ideas, locate general points of agreement (if there are any), and then, with civility, discuss the points on which you disagree. Keep this in mind as you work on your uniform debate.

Someone once said that the mark of an educated person is that he or she can entertain an idea without accepting it.

ANSWER

1. Explain the difference between difference and degree. ______

2. What is an *a fortiori* argument? ______

3. List several ways in which you can explore arguments from degree. ______

4. If "arguments from degree" is the genus, what are some species in this genus? ______

LIST

Review the Common Topics: Thus far, we have discussed three common topics and their subtopics. See how many of these you can list in the spaces provided. For the first common topic, we discussed techniques rather than subtopics, so I have not included subtopics for that one.

1. Common Topic #1: ______
2. Common Topic #2: ______

Subtopics: ______

3. Common Topic #3: ______

Subtopics: ______

ANALYZE

Arguments from Degree: Examine the arguments provided and answer the questions that follow.

1. John Donne's "Death Be Not Proud"

Death be not proud, though some have called thee
Mighty and dreadful, for, thou are not so,
For, those, whom thou think'st, thou dost overthrow,
Die not, poor death, nor yet canst thou kill me.
From rest and sleep, which but thy pictures be,
Much pleasure, then from thee, much more must flow,
And soonest our best men with thee do go,
Rest of their bones and souls delivery.
Thou art slave to Fate, Chance, kings, and desperate men,
And dost with poison, war, and sickness dwell,
And poppy, or charms can make us sleep as well
And better than thy stroke; why swellest thou then?
One short sleep past, we wake eternally,
And death shall be no more; death, thou shalt die.[8]

a. In this poem, John Donne uses an *a fortiori* example to show that death is not as frightful as we think it is. Identify the *a fortiori* argument he uses. To give you a hint, he reasons with his *a fortiori* argument in this manner: "Death is like __________, and we don't fear ___________, so why should we fear death?"

b. What is another example Donne uses to prove that death should not be proud? (Note: This example is not really an *a fortiori* argument.)

ANALYZE

2. Matthew 7:9-11, ASV

Or what man is there of you, who, if his son shall ask him for a loaf, will give him a stone; or if he shall ask for a fish, will give him a serpent? If ye then, being evil, know how to give good gifts unto your children, how much more shall your Father who is in heaven give good things to them that ask him?

a. What is the thesis of this argument from Jesus' Sermon on the Mount? What *a fortiori* example does he give to support his thesis?

b. Does this *a fortiori* argument argue from the weaker to the stronger or the stronger to the weaker?

ANALYZE

3. Matthew 9:1-7, NASB

Getting into a boat, Jesus crossed over the sea and came to His own city. And they brought to Him a paralytic lying on a bed. Seeing their faith, Jesus said to the paralytic, "Take courage, son; your sins are forgiven." And some of the scribes said to themselves, "This fellow blasphemes." And Jesus knowing their thoughts said, "Why are you thinking evil in your hearts? Which is easier, to say, 'Your sins are forgiven,' or to say, 'Get up, and walk'? But so that you may know that the Son of Man has authority on earth to forgive sins"—then He said to the paralytic, "Get up, pick up your bed and go home." And he got up and went home.

a. What is the thesis of Jesus' argument? How does he prove it?

b. Is this a general argument from degree or an *a fortiori* argument? Explain your answer.

BRAINSTORM

Use the provided questions to help you brainstorm arguments from degree for your curfew debate. Then, to support your thesis, write a paragraph that contains an introduction, conclusion, and at least three arguments from degree.

Dress Code and Arguments from Degree:

1. I think we can all agree that promoting a good, ordered learning environment in school is crucial. Given that, how is your dress code proposal better than your opponent's? That is, how does it promote a better school atmosphere?

2. I think we can also agree that encouraging students' individuality and personalities (within the proper boundaries) is important. How does your position allow schools to do this better than your opponent's position does?

3. Another important question you can explore is: Which is more important, creating a good school environment or encouraging a student's individuality? You might also explore if the two positions are mutually exclusive ideas.

4. Examine the list of methods for developing arguments from degree. Choose one of those methods and form an argument from degree.

CHAPTER 13 *Fallacies of Comparison*

Now that we have examined the common topic of comparison, let's look at some common errors you might make as you are constructing an argument using this technique. First, we will examine the most commonly committed fallacy when people do comparisons: false analogy. As you can tell by the name, this is an analogy that just doesn't work. That is, the analogy breaks down because the two examples being compared are too dissimilar. Before I explain this further, it is important for you to know that all analogies break down eventually. Whenever you compare two different items, there will always be some significant dissimilarity. Therefore, it is important that the examples in your analogy are similar in the areas most relevant to your topic.

To better illustrate the fallacy of false analogy, recall the marriage and contract analogies I used as examples for the hypothetical debate on the secession of the South. (Don't remember that one? Go back to chapter 10 to refresh your memory.) Now, consider the following hypothetical analogy for secession: "The South had the right to secede from the North just like a traveler must choose which path to take when he comes to a fork in the road." Although you might be able to make some kind of point from this analogy, it would be a weak one because this is a false analogy. The first two analogies I used were strong because marriages and contracts have moral, ethical and legal implications, making them good comparisons to use when considering whether or not the secession was ethical or just. In contrast, a road, divided or not, possesses no moral or ethical implications. It might be easier or less confusing for the traveler if the road did not divide, but there is nothing moral or immoral about the road. Therefore, it is not a good analogy for a discussion about secession. When you are constructing analogies, make sure that the two items you are comparing are similar in the points most relevant to your argument. In addition, although any two items will have some dissimilarities, make sure none of them are glaring.

Another fallacy to beware of pertains to the subtopic of difference. Make sure that when you are using the subtopic of difference, the difference you are discussing truly exists. Sometimes people make nonexistent distinctions between examples. In this case, they are committing a fallacy of clarity that is called **distinction without difference**. For instance, let's say a mother scolds two brothers for quarreling. If the brothers say, "We're not fighting, we're just expressing our dislike of each other at a very loud volume," this would be an example of distinction without difference. The brothers distinguish what they are doing from fighting, but no true difference actually exists.

The subtopic of degree presents another potential fallacy. You might remember the following method for developing an argument from degree: What the minority of people would choose is better than what the majority of people would choose. If someone uses this argument as an ironclad formula, or without supporting evidence, he might be making a **snob appeal**. When someone commits this fallacy, he argues that his argument is correct because the elite or "the best

people" accept it. For example, you have probably noticed commercials urging you to buy a product, such as a certain type of exquisite chocolate or fine wine, because of its refinement and class. When advertisers do this, they imply that you will exhibit good taste and be one of the "elite" if you choose their product. In order to use the argument of minority over majority properly and avoid snob appeal, you must demonstrate through examples and evidence from legitimate authorities that people with educated taste accept your conclusion and that their acceptance is logical.

For example, if a company advertises that the best athletes prefer its tennis shoes over any other brand, this could be a legitimate argument if, indeed, a majority of seasoned athletes prefer the shoes over the many others they've used. However, if the company does not actually have this experienced clientele and the advertisers make this claim simply to create an elite reputation, they are making a snob appeal. Furthermore, remember that even people of exquisite taste or experience can make mistakes. Therefore, this general rule should not be applied like a formula. For example, you may recall the famous children's story called "The Emperor's New Clothes." In this story, the emperor so desires the most exquisite fashions that two charlatans are able to trick him into wearing "invisible clothes." The tricksters claim that only the most elite, or most intelligent and capable, people can see these fine clothes. Of course, the emperor will not admit he can't see them, and no one else will admit that they cannot see the clothes and, thereby, reveal ignorance. Because of this effective use of snob appeal, the king ends up parading *au natural* (naked) through the city streets.

Lastly, I want to mention the **appeal to moderation**. When people commit an appeal to moderation, they assume that the correct answer is always the middle ground between two extremes. For instance, you might remember that in chapter 11, which discussed the subtopic of difference, I mentioned that people often argue over the best solution to poverty in the United States. Some people argue that the government should provide all the needs of the poor. Other people argue that the poor just need to work harder to raise themselves out of poverty. If a person were to argue that the correct answer is somewhere in the middle, without providing appropriate evidence supporting this claim, he would be committing the fallacy of appeal to moderation. People often commit this fallacy because they are trying to be polite, and they are trying to recognize the positive points on either side of an argument. While people who hold opposing views of an issue may both have good points, it does not automatically mean that the best solution is the middle, or an average, of the different viewpoints. Some people's views may be entirely wrong, or some views might be somewhat right but mostly wrong. It is possible to disagree with someone's viewpoint and still be polite and dignified in an argument. Therefore, you should only claim that the middle between two viewpoints is the correct view if, indeed, the evidence indicates this is so. When I discussed the subtopic of degree, I mentioned that it can help you determine points of agreement with your opponent. However, you should not always assume that there *are* points of agreement. Some arguments may be completely wrong, and you should not pretend otherwise, although you should remain civil in these situations.

As you form your arguments for the uniform debate, remember that your premises should lead as closely as possible to your conclusion. Therefore, as you craft your premises, regularly ask yourself, "Why does this premise support my conclusion?" If you do this regularly, it may help you detect fallacies more easily.

DEFINE

1. False Analogy: ____________________

2. Distinction Without Difference: ____________________

3. Snob Appeal: ____________________

4. Appeal to Moderation: ____________________

IDENTIFY

Fallacies: Read the arguments in this section and determine the fallacies being committed. Also, explain why the fallacy you chose applies to this statement or why the premises of the argument do not lead to the conclusion (premises or conclusions may be implied). Some of these arguments will contain fallacies from previous chapters.

1. A person should care for her health, just like a painter paints a house. When a painter paints a house, he carefully applies the paint and neatly paints the trim. In the same way, people should eat healthfully and exercise.

Fallacy: ____________________

Explanation: ____________________

2. A child says to his mother, who is scolding him for picking on his brother, "I wasn't picking on him. I was just observing some unusual characteristics of his facial structure."

Fallacy: ____________________

Explanation: ____________________

3. You wouldn't enjoy this movie because you lack the proper artistic sensibilities.

Fallacy: ____________________

Explanation: ____________________

IDENTIFY

4. Benjamin Franklin once said, "Don't put off until tomorrow what you can do today." So, even though my birthday is tomorrow, I'm going to eat all of my cake and open my presents today. No one's going to call me a procrastinator.

Fallacy: ______________________________

Explanation: ______________________________

____

____

5. Everyone is voting democrat this election. That is clearly the correct choice.

Fallacy: ______________________________

Explanation: ______________________________

____

____

6. I've been drinking more milk ever since I saw my favorite soccer player in that new milk commercial.

Fallacy: ______________________________

Explanation: ______________________________

____

____

7. A student says to his teacher, "I wasn't cheating! I was just making sure his handwriting was legible."

Fallacy: ______________________________

Explanation: ______________________________

____

____

8. Our new line of gourmet mustard is only for those who can truly recognize excellent quality.

Fallacy: ______________________________

Explanation: ______________________________

____

____

9. A mother said to her son, "You can eat a whole gallon of ice cream in one sitting when you are on your own and pay for your own dental bills." Later, when the boy's parents were on vacation and his grandparents were staying with him, he told his grandma, "Mom said I could eat a whole gallon of ice cream in one sitting."

Fallacy: ______________________________

Explanation: ______________________________

____

____

You are now familiar with the common topic of comparison, its subtopics, and its potential fallacies. Read the following essay, which contains an argument from comparison, and then answer the questions that follow.

I Have a Dream

The following excerpt is from the famous "I Have a Dream Speech" by Martin Luther King, Jr. which was delivered at the Lincoln Memorial in Washington D.C. on August 28, 1963. In this excerpt, note the ways in which King crafts an argument from comparison and then answer the questions that follow.

> In a sense we have come to our nation's capital to cash a check. When the architects of our republic wrote the magnificent words of the Constitution and the Declaration of Independence, they were signing a promissory note to which every American was to fall heir. This note was a promise that all men, yes, black men as well as white men, would be guaranteed the unalienable rights of life, liberty, and the pursuit of happiness.
>
> It is obvious today that America has defaulted on this promissory note insofar as her citizens of color are concerned. Instead of honoring this sacred obligation, America has given the Negro people a bad check, a check which has come back marked "insufficient funds." But we refuse to believe that the bank of justice is bankrupt. We refuse to believe that there are insufficient funds in the great vaults of opportunity of this nation. So we have come to cash this check—a check that will give us upon demand the riches of freedom and the security of justice. We have also come to this hallowed spot to remind America of the fierce urgency of now. This is no time to engage in the luxury of cooling off or to take the tranquilizing drug of gradualism. Now is the time to make real the promises of democracy. Now is the time to rise from the dark and desolate valley of segregation to the sunlit path of racial justice. Now is the time to lift our nation from the quick sands of racial injustice to the solid rock of brotherhood. Now is the time to make justice a reality for all of God's children.[1]

ANSWER

1. Identify the analogy in this essay. ______

2. List two authorities appealed to in this argument. ______

3. List one other topic or subtopic found in this essay. ______

FOLLOW UP

Just as the essay on justice in chapter 9 (see page 70) did, this speech excerpt develops a thesis about an abstract concept using the common topics. Choose from the provided list of abstract concepts and brainstorm ways in which you could use the common topics you have studied up to this point to develop the topic. You may also use one of the topics from the list at the end of the justice essay (punishment, humility, mercy, sacrifice, and forgiveness) or make up one of your own topics.

Abstract Concepts: developing the mind to its full potential; good education; making true friendships; the characteristics of enduring love; the blessing and curse of television; characteristics of excellent movies; the benefit of excellent books

Common Topic 4

Relationship

As you have studied the common topics, you have probably noticed that some of them can help you to explore the different aspects of a concept. For instance, the common topic of definition helps you to explore all of the different ways in which you can define and illustrate a word. The common topic of relationship is another common topic that can help you to discover the various facets of a concept. By examining the ways in which different concepts relate to each other, you can better understand those concepts and thus construct a better argument.

For example, if you were developing an argument for reducing the crime rate in big cities, you would certainly want to define the term "crime." It would also be very important to examine ideas that are related to crime. For instance, you would want to examine the causes of crime and the effects of crime so that you could show the problems that arise from high crime rates. You would also want to discuss concepts that are the results of high crime rates, such as victimization, violence, and fear. Exploring these ideas would also help to illustrate the need for preventing crime. Furthermore, as you were developing this argument about methods for reducing the crime rate in big cities, you would probably examine cities with low or non-existent crime rates. Examining those cities would help you illustrate methods that effectively prevent crime. You would also likely disprove ideas contrary to your thesis, such as the idea that crime is not a significant problem or that it is not possible to prevent high crime rates in big cities. Whenever you explore relationships between ideas or concepts, you are using the common topic of relationship. Carefully studying the common topic of relationship with its various subtopics will help you understand how to accurately determine many important connections between concepts, thereby allowing you to build solid arguments.

The common topic of relationship is broken up into several subtopics, including cause and effect, antecedent and consequence, and contraries and contradictories.

The following is a brief list of definitions for each subtopic of relationship, as well as some fallacies of this common topic.

Cause and Effect: This is one of the most common argument techniques that people use. When someone argues from cause and effect, he argues that A causes B.

The most common fallacy committed with cause and effect arguments is **false cause**. When someone commits false cause, she argues that because A happened before B, A caused B. This is a problematic argument because it can be applied to many events that are not causally connected. ***Post hoc ergo propter hoc*** is a common Latin name used for this fallacy. Another closely related fallacy is the fallacy of **slippery slope**. It is a fallacy in which it is assumed that one step in a given direction will lead much further down that same path, without any argument being given as to why one thing will lead to another.

Antecedent and Consequence: When someone uses the subtopic of antecedent and consequence, he demonstrates that when A is present, B naturally follows.

Contraries: The contrary of a statement is the exact opposite. For instance, if I were to say, "Exercise is a healthy hobby," the contrary of this statement would be "Exercise is an unhealthy hobby." The contrary statement to your thesis will contain the antonym (a word of opposite meaning) of the key word in your statement. When you disprove the contrary statement of your thesis statement, it can increase the credibility of your thesis.

Contradictories: Contradictories deny a statement altogether. Contradictory statements have the word "not" in the second part of a statement, usually preceding an adjective or verb. For instance, the contradictory of the statement "Exercise is a healthy hobby" is "Exercise is not a healthy hobby."

The topic of relationship demonstrates that when we explore examples and ideas related to our topic in some way, it can clarify and support our ideas. Not only that, the result or consequence of an idea often determines the worth of that idea. Relationship helps us explore these possible outcomes.

The subtopic of cause and effect is the most common subtopic of relationship. This subtopic uses an argument technique that draws a conclusion by demonstrating that one phenomenon caused another phenomenon to occur. If you listen to people long enough, you will realize that they hold many beliefs about the causes of certain phenomena. For instance, people generally believe that talking on cell phones while driving can cause accidents; that not wearing warm enough clothing in cold weather can cause colds; and that eating too much sugar can cause tooth decay. In fact, people have heard these ideas with such frequency that they accept them as common wisdom. However, too often people are quick to assume causal connections between events or ideas that are closely associated or that occur in close proximity to one another. Upon further examination, "close association" or "proximity" often do not imply the connection that you might initially think is indicated. For example, physicians once believed that bad blood caused sickness. Therefore, when someone had a severe sickness, doctors would cut them to drain the bad blood.[1] At the time, this seemed like a logical causal connection, likely because it sometimes seemed to bring about good results, but later scientific research disproved this theory. This example demonstrates that determining the relationship between two ideas can be more difficult than it seems.

Another example of this can be found in Mark Twain's book *The Prince and the Pauper*, which is set seventeenth-century Tudor England. There is a scene in the book in which local magistrates drag two women accused of witchcraft before the king. When the king asks for evidence indicating the women's supernatural power, the magistrates claim that the two women caused a storm that destroyed their neighbor's crops. Impressed with this supposed power, the king demands to know the method by which the women accomplished this powerful act. The accusers state that the women pulled off their socks, and, suddenly, a storm blew in, destroying the crops. Obviously, these magistrates assumed a faulty causal relationship that because the women removed their socks, and a storm blew in, the sock removal caused the storm. As ridiculous as it may seem, scenarios like this were all too common in more superstitious times. However, although we may recognize the absurdity of believing such a bizarre causal connection, many people still struggle with determining accurate causality.

John Stuart Mill, who lived from 1800 to 1873, was a scholar and logician who established several methods for accurately determining these relationships. Mill was a child prodigy (child genius). By the age of fourteen, he had learned Latin, read most classical literary works, and had a thorough foundation in other subjects like logic, political economy, history, and mathematics.[2] In 1843, Mill, recognizing a need for a way to accurately determine causal relationships, wrote a book called *System of Logic* in which he discussed several tests a person could use to determine causality. These tests are the **method of agreement**, the **method of difference**, the joint **method of agreement and difference**, the **method of residues**, and the **method of concomitant variance**. Some of these terms may seem a little intimidating, but they are actually easy to understand, and they provide helpful guidance for understanding causal relationships.[3]

When people use the method of agreement, they look at many examples to determine a common factor that is causing a shared characteristic. Imagine that an unusually high number of people in a certain city contract leukemia. Researchers might thoroughly interview all of the people in that city to discover a common factor causing the leukemia. For instance, after interviewing hundreds of sick people in the city, the researchers might discover three common characteristics: all of the sick people drink the same water, eat vegetables sprayed by a particular pesticide, and use a locally sold cleaning solution. Once the researchers determine these common factors, they will try to determine which factor or combination of factors is making people sick. This is the method of agreement.[4]

The method of difference uses the opposite approach. When people use this method, they compare examples with a certain characteristic to examples that do not have this characteristic. Through this method, they determine the factor that is present with the characteristic and absent without it.[5] For example, if researchers wished to use this method to determine the cause of leukemia mentioned in the previous paragraph, they might compare the sick people in the city with the healthy people in the city, or to people in another city with low rates of leukemia, in order to determine the factor that is present with the sick people but absent in healthy people or in people outside of the city. In this case, the researchers examine factors that differ between sick people and healthy people.

The method of agreement and difference is exactly what its name implies: a combination of the methods of agreement and difference. For example, if the leukemia researchers used this method, they would examine every sick person in the city to determine the common causal factor, *and* they would also examine the healthy city people or healthy people in different cities to determine the factors that are different. If the researchers used both of the methods of agreement and difference, it might help them find the cause more quickly.[6]

The method of agreement and difference is exactly what its name implies: a combination of the methods of agreement and difference.

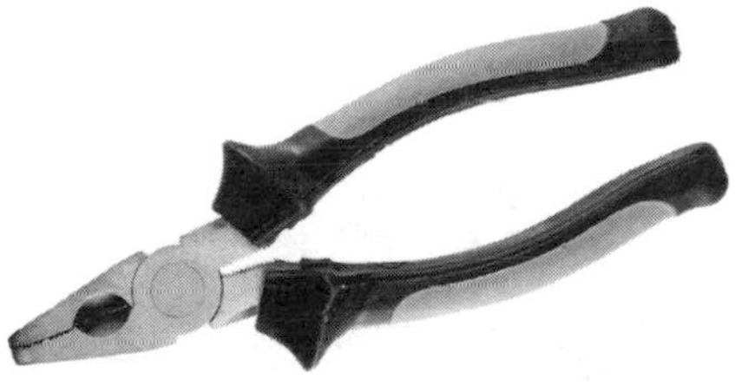

The name "method of residues" sounds intimidating, but it is not. A residue is something that is left over. For instance, if a muddy stream overflows its bank and flows through someone's yard, the stream will leave a "residue" of mud when it returns to its normal level. We could rename the method of residue the "method of leftovers." When researchers use this method, they hypothesize several factors that are likely causal factors for a phenomenon. Then, through research and experimentation, they systematically eliminate unlikely causal factors until they are left with a possible causal factor that is difficult to eliminate. This leftover (the residual factor) will be the most probable causal factor.

For example, the leukemia researchers might hypothesize that the most likely causal factors for the high levels of leukemia in the city are the water, the air, a locally sold cleaning solution, or a pesticide used in higher concentration in this area. They will perform many tests on each of these possible factors to determine the likelihood of each of them as a causal factor for leukemia. Through these tests, they will be able to eliminate some of these factors as possible causal agents. Once they discard the least probable causes, they will be able to focus more seriously on the most likely cause and hopefully find a solution to the problem

The last method John Stuart Mill devised for testing causal connections is the method of concomitant variance. It may help you to think of the method of concomitant variance as the "spiral method." When researchers or logicians use this method, they observe interconnections between two phenomena. That is, they notice that as one phenomenon increases or decreases, the other increases or decreases simultaneously. It will appear as though these factors are so interconnected, as though bound into a spiral, that it is impossible for one to increase or decrease without the other. Sometimes, one phenomenon may increase at the same rate at which the other decreases, or vice versa, but this still demonstrates the same interconnection.

We can find some good examples for this "spiral effect" in life. As mentioned previously, researchers have noticed several such factors that seem to be linked together. For instance, the more education a person has, the more money they make.[7] Researchers have also recently determined that the more people take afternoon naps, the less likely they are to have heart disease.[8] When researchers use the method of concomitant variance, they identify phenomena that seem to change simultaneously because this can indicate a link between the two phenomena.

When a cause is sufficient, it means that the cause can bring about a desired effect.

Mill's methods may seem like common sense, but common sense is not as common as it may seem. Often a connection is clear only after someone points it out. In addition, as you saw previously when you examined the idols of the tribe (see chapter 2), humans are quick to make unwarranted conclusions. Therefore, by applying Mill's methods, you will be able to fully utilize your common sense and to make careful and reasonable conclusions about causal relationships.

Before we use causal arguments to support the curfew argument, we should discuss the difference between a **sufficient cause** and a **necessary cause**. When a cause is sufficient, it means that the cause can bring about a desired effect. For instance, we know that if someone is out in the cold for long periods of time without protection, this can cause her to get sick. Being unprotected out in the cold is a sufficient cause. However, it is not a necessary cause. People can get sick even if they never leave their houses. For instance, stress, a weakened immune system, a viral infection, or a genetic abnormality can all cause sickness. Therefore, although being outside in the cold may cause sickness, it is not a necessary cause for sickness.

On the other hand, intelligence is not only a sufficient cause to score 100 percent on an achievement test, it is a necessary cause. It is impossible to score perfect on such a test without some intelligence (unless someone cheated). As another example, consider that an object like a ball or a car will not move of its own accord. It must have a natural or mechanical "mover" or catalyst (like a person or an electrical impulse) to cause it to move. Therefore, a catalyst is not only a sufficient cause for motion, it is also a necessary cause. To summarize, a sufficient cause *may* be present with a phenomenon. A necessary cause *must* be present in order for the phenomenon to occur. It is important to differentiate between sufficient and necessary causes because confusing the two can cause logical error.[9]

Now let's get back to the curfew debate. Previously you have argued that a more lenient curfew will cause increased responsibility. It is important for you to admit that a more lenient or flexible curfew is a sufficient but not necessary cause for increased responsibility. There are many teenagers who are responsible despite strict curfews, and you must admit that some irresponsible teenagers have lenient curfews. Therefore, a flexible curfew is not a necessary cause for responsibility. Remember, don't try to prove a cause necessary when it is only sufficient.

However, you can still use the subtopic of cause and effect to bolster your argument. For instance, you might argue that as you have observed older, more responsible teenagers, you have noticed that all of them work with their parents to establish good personal guidelines. That is, the teenagers take responsibility for their own personal well-being. Therefore, because the parents trust their teenagers' wisdom and decision-making skills, they are willing to negotiate rules that will accomplish shared goals, such as responsibility and safety.

It is important to recognize that although "rule negotiation" is a common factor with all of these teenagers, they also share several other common factors: they are wise, mature, and disciplined teens who are respectful to their parents. If you are using the subtopic of cause and effect responsibly, you can point out that the "rule negotiation" is not the sole causal factor of the teens' responsibility. The teenager's wisdom and discipline are also factors. If you realize this, you will understand that you must prove to your parents that you respect them and the discipline and wisdom they have taught you.

At this point, you should recognize that you have come a long way from the beginning of this discussion when you might have considered moping or throwing a tantrum in response to your parents' curfew rules. You are starting to think in a deep, sophisticated manner, and are able to understand and respect your parents' point of view as well. Remember that one mark of a good logician is the ability to properly evaluate, and even appreciate, an opposing opinion.

EXPLAIN

1. Who is John Stuart Mill and why is he important in a chapter discussing cause and effect?

DESCRIBE

Give a description of each of the provided methods Mill suggested to test cause and effect.

1. Method of Agreement:

2. Method of Difference:

3. Method of Agreement and Difference:

4. Method of Residues:

5. Method of Concomitant Variance:

DIFFERENTIATE

Explain the difference between a necessary cause and a sufficient cause.

ANSWER

Famous Arguments from Cause and Effect: Read the provided arguments and answer the questions that follow.

1. From Edmund Burke's "Conciliation with America"

> Do you imagine, then, that it is the land tax which raises your revenue, that it is the annual vote in the committee of supply which gives you your army? No! Surely not! It is the love of the people; it is their attachment to their government, from the deep stake they have in such a glorious institution.[10]

1. What, according to Burke, is the cause of England's increased revenue?

2. What does the crown seem to believe is the cause of this raised revenue?

3. What is Burke's implied thesis here?

4. This excerpt is very short. What examples from history can you think of that might have further proven Burke's point? (If you are having problems thinking of one, research the history of the Magna Carta and explain how this historical incident could support Burke's argument).

ANSWER

2. From Thomas Aquinas' "Arguments from the Existence of God"

In the world of sense we find there is an order of efficient cause. There is no case known (nor, indeed, is it possible) in which a thing is found to be the efficient cause of itself, because in that case it would be prior to itself, which is impossible. Now in efficient causes it is not possible to go on to infinity, because in all efficient causes following in order, the first is the cause of the intermediate cause, and the intermediate is the cause of the ultimate cause, whether the intermediate cause be several, or one only. Now to take away the cause is to take away the effect. Therefore, if there be no first cause among efficient causes, there will be no ultimate, nor any intermediate cause. But if in efficient causes it is possible to go on to infinity, there will be no first efficient cause, neither will there be an ultimate effect, nor any intermediate efficient causes, all of which is plainly false. Therefore, it is necessary to admit a first efficient cause. To which everyone gives the name of God.[11]

1. State Aquinas' thesis in your own words. ______________________________

2. What cause and effect relationship does he state to support his thesis? ______________________________

3. What other example could you use to support such a thesis? ______________________________

REVIEW

Arguments from Statistics and Authority: In the body of this chapter, I mentioned an article that claimed that taking regular afternoon naps reduces heart disease. Access and read this article online at: <http://www.digitaljournal.com/article/113290/Regular_naps_good_for_your_heart> (or find a similar article online that makes this claim). Then, write a brief paragraph on the strengths and weaknesses of the statistics and the authorities presented as evidence for this conclusion.

BRAINSTORM

Uniforms and Arguments from Cause and Effect: Employ the subtopic of cause and effect to brainstorm arguments for your thesis. Use the provided questions to get started and then write a paragraph that develops your argument.

1. What are several outcomes, or effects, of adopting a uniform? Is adopting a uniform a necessary or sufficient cause for this effect? How does this support or contradict your thesis?

2. What are several outcomes, or effects, of not adopting a uniform? Is not having a uniform a necessary or sufficient cause for this effect? How does this support or contradict your thesis?

3. Consider several schools that have a good atmosphere. Could you use any of Mill's methods to determine that having a school uniform or not having a school uniform was a possible cause of this good atmosphere?

4. Can you think of several schools that have a bad atmosphere? Could you use any of Mill's methods to determine that not having a school uniform or having a school uniform led to this bad atmosphere?

5. Remember that just because something is a sufficient cause rather than a necessary cause doesn't mean that you cannot use it in your argument. Sufficient causes are important causes to consider; just don't confuse them with necessary causes or try to prove that it's a necessary cause when you know otherwise.

CHAPTER 16 *Subtopic: Antecedent and Consequence*

Although the subtopic of antecedent and consequence may seem identical to that of cause and effect, it is actually quite different. While the subtopic of cause and effect discusses the consequences of a situation or action, the subtopic of antecedent and consequence focuses on what naturally happens as a result of an action or situation. For example, someone might argue from the subtopic of cause and effect that studying hard will result in good grades or that running a lot will result in increased cardiovascular fitness. Someone arguing from the subtopic of antecedent and consequence would focus on what naturally follows from the fact that someone is a student or a runner. For example, an argument from antecedent and consequence would be formed this way: Given that someone is a student, it follows that he will learn new facts, think critically, and challenge his mind. Or, given that someone is a runner, it follows that he will have tennis shoes and that he will practice running several times a week.

When you use the subtopic of antecedent and consequence, it can help you to demonstrate the logical conclusion of a belief or an action. Let's look at a few more examples of this subtopic. Given that a person is a United States citizen, it follows that she is guaranteed certain constitutional rights, such as freedom of speech and religion. Or, given that someone can speak Spanish and English, it follows that he will travel more easily in Spain and Mexico than his friends who only speak English. Susan B. Anthony's argument for women's suffrage, which we examined in the review exercises of chapter 3, contained arguments from antecedent and consequence based on her definition of "citizen." She argued that certain rights and responsibilities proceed from being a citizen, and then she demonstrated that women are citizens. In her argument, her antecedent was "being a citizen," and she argued that the consequence, which was the right to vote, proceeded from that antecedent.

When someone uses the subtopic of antecedent and consequence, he argues, "Given A, B follows." The following are some examples of antecedent and consequence statements:

Given that you are an American, it follows that you have the right of freedom of speech and freedom of religion.

Given that you are a student, it follows that you should be learning new ideas and skills each year.

Given that you are a sibling, you have a brother or a sister.

If you are thinking that these statements seem like common sense, you are correct. Certainly the statements of antecedent and consequence are somewhat obvious, but these arguments can indicate obvious ideas that we might unwittingly neglect when forming arguments. They can also help us discover ideas that are not readily apparent.

For example, if you are like many teenagers, you might feel sometimes that you are abnormal because to you life seems a lot harder than it should be. You might feel that if you could just find the right formula for life, everything would run smoothly. Using the subtopic of antecedent and consequence might help you think more clearly about this. You might reason about your life in this way: "Given that I am a teenager, it follows that I am in a youthful state, or condition, moving toward adulthood. Given that I am moving from one state to another, it follows that this will cause some change and challenge in my life. Change and challenge usually involve some level of discomfort and pain. Therefore, it follows that, since experiencing some discomfort in life is a normal part of growing up, there is nothing wrong with me." You will notice that with this line of reasoning, I used definitions in addition to several antecedent and consequence arguments.

How could you use this subtopic in your curfew argument? Let's start with the fact that you are a young adult. This is the antecedent. What are the consequences of your young adulthood? There are several. Given that you are a young adult, it follows that you will have both restrictions and freedoms. Given that you have this balance of restriction and freedom in your life, it follows that there will be some tension between these two sides of your reality. Also, given that you are a young adult, it follows that you need increasing freedom so that you can learn from your mistakes while you are still in a safe environment. As you practice managing increasing freedom, you will naturally make some mistakes. Some of these mistakes could entail personal injury or harm. Another antecedent that coincides with what has been stated so far is: Given that your parents are your guardians, they feel a responsibility to protect you. They also feel responsible to help mold you into a responsible adult. Given these facts, they know they must let you make some mistakes so that you can adapt to the world.

As you think through these various antecedents and consequences, you should realize that your parents are trying to figure out which mistakes are safe to let you make at this time. You should also realize that higher levels of freedom also entail higher levels of risk. These realizations may give you the patience, respect, and caution you need to discuss this issue successfully with your parents. You may also realize that given that you are a teenager, you have many years ahead of you in which you will have no curfew rules. This conclusion can help relieve some of the stress you may feel at the thought that your parents may reject your curfew proposal.

The subtopic of antecedent and consequence can be very enlightening because it can help you realize implications and consequences of your topic that you have not previously considered. To use this subtopic effectively, select part of your topic and ask yourself questions that help you explore antecedents and consequences. Usually the best way to do this is to ask: Given this antecedent, what follows? This question will lead you to other questions, and as you go through this questioning process, you will realize implications that will aid in developing your thesis statement.

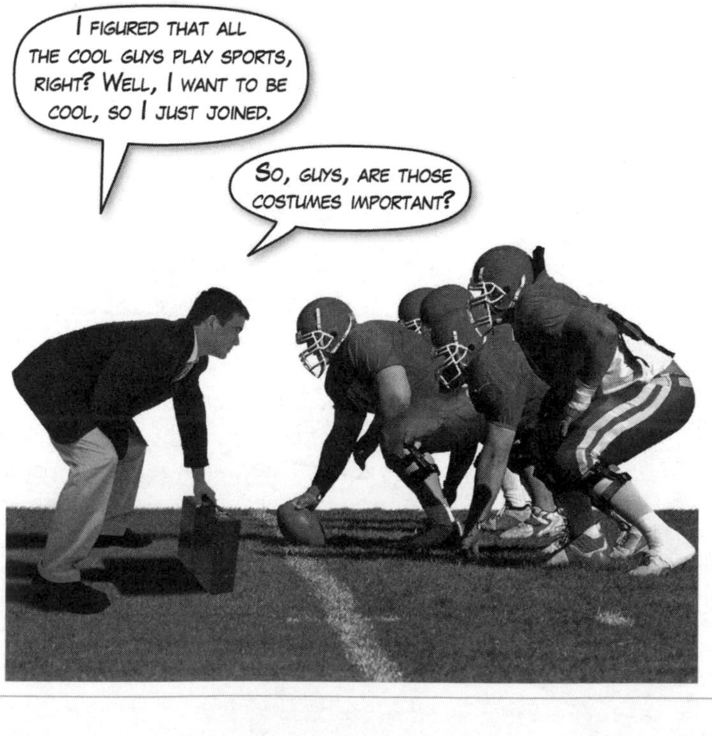

EXPLAIN

1. Explain the common topic of antecedent and consequence. ______________________________

2. Explain how antecedent and consequence is different from cause and effect. ______________

PRACTICE

Antecedent and Consequence: For each of the provided antecedents, explain three consequences that follow. Note that the consequences may be negative, positive, both negative and positive, or neutral.

1. Antecedent: Given that a student reads a lot of books…

Consequence 1: ______________________________

Consequence 2: ______________________________

Consequence 3: ______________________________

2. Antecedent: Given that a person is accident prone…

Consequence 1: ______________________________

Consequence 2: ______________________________

Consequence 3: ______________________________

3. Antecedent: Given that a person lives in a small home…

Consequence 1: ______________________________

Consequence 2: ______________________________

Consequence 3: ______________________________

BRAINSTORM

Choose one of the provided antecedents and come up with three consequences for it:

1. Given that a person is young…
2. Given that a person is old…
3. Given that a person is from a large family…
4. Given that a person is from a small family…
5. Given that a person lives in the South (or North, West, or East)…

Consequence 1: ______________________________

____

Consequence 2: ______________________________

____

Consequence 3: ______________________________

____

DEVELOP

Antecedent and Consequence: Using one of the antecedents from the previous exercise, write a paragraph that contains at least three consequences and that proves something about the antecedent.

____

1. From Thomas Aquinas' "Arguments for the Existence of God"

The first and more manifest way [to argue for the existence of God] is the argument from motion. It is certain, and evident to our senses, that in this world some things are in motion. Now whatever is in motion is put in motion by another, for nothing can be in motion unless it is in potency towards that which it is in motion. But a thing moves in so far as it is in act. For motion is nothing else than the reduction of something from potency to act. But nothing can be reduced from potency to act except by something in a state of act. Thus that which is actually hot, as fire, makes wood, which is potentially hot, to be actually hot, and therefore moves and changes it. Now it is not possible that the same thing should be at once in act and potency in the same respect, but only in different respects. For what is actually hot cannot simultaneously be potentially hot, though it is simultaneously potentially cold. It is therefore impossible that in the same respect and in the same way a thing should be both mover and moved, that is that it should move itself. Therefore, whatever is moved must be moved by another. If that by which it is moved by another, and that by another again. But this cannot go on to infinity, because then there would be no first mover, and, consequently, no other mover, seeing that subsequent movers move only because as they are moved by the first mover, just as the staff moves only because it is moved by the hand. Therefore it is necessary to arrive at a first mover which is moved by no other. And this everyone understands to be God.[1]

a. What is the thesis of this excerpt? ____

____

____

____

____

b. What is the antecedent and consequence argument used in this excerpt?______________

____

____

____

____

____

____

____

____

EXAMINE

Famous Arguments: Read each of the provided excerpts and then answer the questions that follow. Remember that some of these excerpts use challenging or difficult language, and you may need to read them slowly and more than once to understand them.

EXAMINE

2. From Montaigne's "That to Study Philosophy Is to Learn to Die"

Cicero says "that to study philosophy is nothing but to prepare one's self to die." The reason of which is, because study and contemplation do in some sort withdraw from us our soul, and employ it separately from the body, which is a kind of apprenticeship and a resemblance of death; or else, because all the wisdom and reasoning in the world do in the end conclude in this point, to teach us not to fear to die. And to say the truth, either our reason mocks us, or it ought to have no other aim but our contentment only, nor to endeavour anything but, in sum, to make us live well, and, as the Holy Scripture says, at our ease. All the opinions of the world agree in this, that pleasure is our end, though we make use of divers means to attain it: They would, otherwise, be rejected at the first motion; for who would give ear to him that should propose affliction and misery for his end.[2]

a. What is the thesis of this excerpt? ______________________________

____

____

____

b. What is the antecedent and consequence argument used in this excerpt? ______________________________

____

____

____

c. What other common topic (or subtopic) does Montaigne use in this excerpt? ______________________________

____

____

____

____

____

____

EXAMINE

3. *From Montaigne's "That the Profit of One Man Is the Damage of Another"*

Demades the Athenian condemned one of his city, whose trade it was to sell the necessaries for funeral ceremonies, upon pretence that he demanded unreasonable profit, and that that profit could not accrue to him but by the death of a great number of people. A judgment that appears to be ill grounded, forasmuch as no profit whatever can possibly be made but at that expense of another, and that by the same rule he should condemn all gain of what kind soever. The merchant only thrives by the debauchery of youth; the husbandman by the dearness of grain; the architect by the ruin of buildings; lawyers, and officers of justice, by the suits and contentions of men; nay, even the hour and office of divines are derived form our death and vices. A physician takes no pleasure in the health of even of his friends, says the ancient Greek comic writer, nor a soldier in the peace of his country, and so of the rest.[3]

a. What is the thesis of this excerpt? ______________________________

____

____

____

b. What is the antecedent and consequence argument used in this excerpt? ______________________________

____

____

____

c. What other common topic (or subtopic) does Montaigne use in this excerpt? ______________________________

____

____

____

____

____

____

EXAMINE

4. From Montaigne's "Of Ancient Customs"

Now, seeing that our change of fashions is so prompt and sudden, that the inventions of all the tailors in the world cannot furnish out new whim-whams enow to feed our vanity withal, there will often be a necessity that the despised forms must again come in vogue, and these immediately after fall into the same contempt; and that the same judgment must, in the space of fifteen or twenty years, take up half-a-dozen not only diverse but contrary opinions, with an incredible lightness and inconstancy; there is not any of us discreet, who suffers not himself to be gulled with this contradiction, and both in external and internal sights to be insensible blinded.[4]

a. What is the thesis of this excerpt? ______________________________

____

____

____

b. What is the antecedent and consequence argument used in this excerpt?______________________________

____

____

____

c. Determine two other common topics (or subtopics) that you could use to support Montaigne's thesis and write several sentences developing his argument with those common topics (or subtopics).

____

____

____

____

____

EXAMINE

5. From Montaigne's "Of Prayers"

I know not if or no I am wrong; but since, by a particular favor of the divine bounty, a certain form of prayer has been prescribed and dictated to us, word by word, from the mouth of God Himself, I have ever been of opinion that we ought to have it in more frequent use that we yet have; and if I were worthy to advise, at the sitting down to and rising from our tables, at our rising from and going to bed, and in every particular action wherein prayer is used, I would that Christians always make use of the Lord's prayer, of not alone, yet at least always.[5]

a. What is the thesis of this excerpt? ____

____

____

____

b. What is the antecedent and consequence argument used in this excerpt?_______________

____

____

____

c. Determine two other common topics (or subtopics) that you could use to support Montaigne's thesis and write several sentences developing his argument with those common topics (or subtopics).

____

____

____

____

____

____

EXPLORE

Uniforms and Arguments from Antecedent and Consequence: Use the provided questions to help you explore some ways you could use the subtopic of antecedent and consequence to prove your point.

1. Below is a list of some possible antecedents related to uniforms. Choose at least two that seem like they might support your thesis and brainstorm several consequences for them.

Given that a student is in school…

Given that students are young…

Given that administrators and teachers are older…

Given that uniforms require a certain standard of dress…

Given that uniforms standardize appearance…

Given that a school has no uniforms…

Given that a school has uniforms…

2. Think of two other antecedents related to this debate and write two consequences for them.

CHAPTER 17 *Subtopics: Contraries and Contradictories*

Sometimes the best way to explore a subject is by examining its opposite or a negative form of it. For instance, let's say that your class is debating the following thesis statement: Chewing gum in school improves student concentration. Of course, you can use the common topics of definition, comparison, and testimony to support this thesis statement, but you could also explore the opposite (contrary) or negative (contradictory) form of it. This is what the contrary and contradictory of the above thesis statement look like:

Contrary: Chewing gum in school decreases student concentration.

Contradictory: Chewing gum in school does not improve student concentration.

At first glance, these statements may seem identical, but they are slightly different and therefore may generate different arguments. The first statement, the contrary, states that gum chewing has the opposite effect on student concentration than what the thesis statement claims. The second sentence, the contradictory, completely denies the thesis statement. Let's look at the first statement: Chewing gum in school *decreases* student concentration. Notice that the contrary statement is a completely opposite idea to that of the original thesis statement. It contains the antonym—"decreases"—of the key word in the original thesis statement—"improves". Consider another thesis statement: "School uniforms promote an *ordered* learning environment." The contrary statement to this thesis would be: "School uniforms promote a *disordered* learning environment." Notice that the italicized words are antonyms, or opposites, of the key word presented in the thesis statements.

When you prove the contrary of your thesis statement, it can help support your idea. For instance, if you want to disprove the contrary statement of the gum thesis, you might write something like this: Some people believe that chewing gum in school decreases student concentration. However, this is incorrect. When students chew gum in a normal manner and do not blow bubbles, it is a silent, mindless activity that does not detract from any other activity. It takes no special skill or concentration to chew gum. Therefore, it does not decrease concentration on any other activity. You have not yet proven that chewing gum improves concentration. However, now that you have proven that it does not *decrease* concentration, you can focus on supporting your thesis, which proposes that it can actually increase student concentration.

The second statement: "Chewing gum in school does *not* improve student concentration" is a contradictory statement. To form the contradictory statement of your thesis, you add the word "not" before the second part of the sentence, usually before an adjective or a verb phrase. Let's say your thesis statement was: "School uniforms promote an ordered learning atmosphere." The contradictory statement to this is: "School uniforms do *not* promote an ordered learning atmosphere." Notice the "not" in the second half of the sentence right before the verb "promote." In the example above, the contradictory statement of "Chewing gum in school improves student concentration" is "Chewing gum in school *does not* improve student concentration."

If you want to use the contradictory gum statement to support your thesis statement, this is how you might write it: Some people believe that chewing gum in school does not improve student concentration, but this is incorrect. Many students find that chewing gum helps them pay attention. School requires students to sit still at their desks for long periods of time, which can make many students extremely restless. Chewing gum is a non-distracting method for a student to relieve tension so that he or she can concentrate more fully. In this short paragraph, you disprove the contradictory of your thesis statement. By doing this, you supported your thesis statement that chewing gum improves student concentration.

We can learn just as much about studying the opposite of our subject as we can by studying the subject itself.

Let's apply the subtopics of contraries and contradictories to your curfew debate. Your thesis statement is: A negotiable, 12:00 a.m. weekend curfew teaches a young adult responsibility. The following are the contrary and contradictory statements for this thesis:

Contrary: A negotiable, 12:00 a.m. weekend curfew teaches a young adult *irresponsibility*.

Contradictory: A negotiable, 12:00 a.m. weekend curfew *does not* teach a young adult responsibility.

To use these statements to support your thesis statement, you must demonstrate that they are false. For example, to use the contrary statement appropriately, you could write the following: Some people believe that a negotiable, 12:00 a.m. weekend curfew teaches a young adult irresponsibility. This is untrue. Although it is true that some students with late curfews engage in irresponsible behavior, such as drinking and reckless driving, it is not the curfew that causes this behavior, but a young adult's predisposition to this behavior. In fact, if a teenager wants to misbehave, he can do so with or without a curfew.

To use the contradictory statement appropriately, you might write this: Although some may believe that a negotiable 12:00 a.m. weekend curfew does not teach a young adult responsibility, there is reason to believe it actually does. If the teenager knows that she can earn more privileges through obeying her curfew, this gives her greater incentive for obedience. In addition, when a young adult shares in rulemaking with her parents, it gives her a sense of pride and responsibility and can improve her relationship with her parents.

The subtopic of contraries and contradictories reminds us that we can learn just as much about studying the opposite of our subject as we can by studying the subject itself. This is why the common topics are so effective. As you have probably realized, this method of argument discovery pushes us to consider possible arguments that we would not otherwise consider. As you use the common topics regularly, you will become a more sophisticated and thorough thinker, which is an excellent sign of logical maturation. Aristotle would be proud of you.

ANSWER

1. What is the difference between contrary and contradictory statements? ____________________

____

____

____

____

____

ANALYZE

Arguments with Contraries and Contradictories: Read the provided excerpts and answer the questions that follow.

Note: Before you read this first excerpt by Thomas Aquinas, it may help you to know that Aquinas wrote a famous book called *Summa Theologica* in which he thoroughly explored Christian theology. This excerpt follows a common pattern in Aquinas' book in which he states a thesis, provides evidence to support this thesis, and then provides evidence that counteracts the thesis. This pattern uses contraries and contradictories. Also note that this first excerpt uses the definition technique of genus and species, which we discussed in chapter 3. If you have forgotten how this technique works, you may want to review that chapter so that you understand this excerpt more thoroughly.

1. From Thomas Aquinas' "Whether God Is Contained in a Genus?"

> *We proceed thus to the Fifth Article*: It seems that God is contained in a genus.
>
> *Objection 1*. For a substance is a being that subsists of itself. But this is especially true of God. Therefore God is in the genus of substance.
>
> *Objection 2*. Further, nothing can be measured save by something of its own genus; as length is measured by length and numbers by number. But God is the measure of all substances, as the Commentator shows (Metaph. X). Therefore, God is the genus of substance.
>
> *On the contrary*, in the intellect, genus is prior to what it contains. But nothing is prior to God either really or in the intellect. Therefore God is not in any genus.[1]

a. What is Aquinas' first thesis? ____

____

____

____

b. What contradictory statement eventually becomes his thesis? ____________________

____

____

____

____

____

ANALYZE

2. From Thomas Aquinas' "Whether God Is Perfect?"

Article I. Whether God Is Perfect?

We proceed thus to the First Article: It seems that to be perfect does not belong to God.

Objection 1. For we say a thing is perfect if it is completely made. But it does not befit God to be made. Therefore He is not perfect.

Objection 2. Further, God is the first beginning of things. But the beginnings of things seem to be imperfect, as seed is the beginning of animal and vegetable life. Therefore God is imperfect.

Objection 3. Further, as shown above (Q. III, A. 4) God's essence is being itself. But being itself seems most imperfect, since it is most general and receptive of all addition. Therefore, God is imperfect.

On the contrary, It is written: Be you perfect as also your heavenly Father is perfect (Matt. 5:48).

I answer that, as the Philosopher relates some ancient philosophers, namely, the Pythagoreans, and Leucippus, did not attribute "best" and "most perfect" to the first principle. The reason was that the ancient philosophers considered only a material principle, and a first principle is most imperfect. For since matter as such is in potency, the first material principle must be potential in the highest degree, and thus most imperfect. Now God is the first principle, not material, but in the order of efficient cause, which must be most perfect. For just as matter, as such, is in potency, an agent, as such, is in act. Hence, the first active principle must be most actual, and therefore most perfect; for a thing is said to be perfect as it is in act, because we call that perfect which lacks nothing of the mode of its perfection.[2]

a. What is Aquinas' initial thesis statement? ______________________________

____

____

____

b. What contrary statement does he eventually accept? ______________________

____

____

____

c. What other common topic does Aquinas use to develop this argument? __________

____

____

____

____

____

____

ANALYZE

3. From Thomas Paine's "Common Sense"

Note: Thomas Paine was famous for advocating the American colonists' rebellion, which eventually led to the Revolutionary War.

> I have heard it asserted by some, that as America has flourished under her former connection with Great Britain, the same connection is necessary towards her future happiness, and will always have the same effect. Nothing can be more fallacious than this kind of argument. We may as well assert that because a child has thrived upon milk, that it is never to have meat, or that the first twenty years of our lives is to become a precedent for the next twenty. But even this is admitting more than is true; for I answer roundly that America would have flourished as much, as probably much more, had no European power taken any notice of her. The commerce by which she hath enriched herself are the necessaries of life, and will always have a market while eating is the custom of Europe.[3]

a. What is the thesis of Paine's argument? ________________________

b. Write the contradictory and contrary statements implied in this argument. ____________

c. What other common topic does Paine use to develop his argument? ____________

PRACTICE

Writing Contrary and Contradictory Statements: Practice writing contrary and contradictory statements for the provided thesis statements.

1. War is the cause of misery in the world.

Contrary: ______________________________

____

____

Contradictory: ______________________________

____

____

2. Good people skills are crucial for success in the world.

Contrary: ______________________________

____

____

Contradictory: ______________________________

____

____

3. Wealth guarantees happiness.

Contrary: ______________________________

____

____

Contradictory: ______________________________

____

____

4. There is such a thing as a benevolent dictator.

Contrary: ______________________________

____

____

Contradictory: ______________________________

____

____

EXPLORE

Arguments with Contraries and Contradictories: Choose one of the statements from the previous review exercise and write a paragraph that explores the contrary or contradictory of that statement by using three common topics.

WRITE

Uniforms and Arguments from Contraries and Contradictories: In the space provided or on a separate piece of paper, write your thesis statement for uniforms. Then, write the contrary and contradictory of that statement. Choose either the contrary or the contradictory statement and then write a paragraph that uses three of the common topics to develop the contrary or contradictory statement into an argument.

CHAPTER 18 *Fallacies of Relationship*

Because the subtopic of cause and effect is one of the most common argument techniques used, most relationship fallacies usually occur when someone tries to prove cause and effect. The two most common relationship fallacies are false cause and slippery slope.

Before we discuss these two fallacies, let me give you a *caveat emptor*, or a caution (from the Latin, "Let the buyer beware"). It can be very difficult to establish causality between two events or things because often an effect has multiple causes. A familiar example might help to illustrate this. Many of you have probably done a science fair project in which you were trying to find out what factor caused a certain effect. For example, you may have tested several different types of plant food to determine which one helped plants to grow best. Your hypothesis was probably something like this: "Plant food A will cause my plants to grow the greatest amount in four weeks." When you are doing a controlled science fair project like this, it is fairly easy to prove a causal relationship, but you still had to try to control all the other possible causal factors. For instance, you had to make sure that the plants all received the same amount of light and fresh air, and you had to make sure that the amount of plant food you gave to the plants was equal. If you were not careful about these other factors, they may have interfered with your hypothesis. For example, if one of your plants was in a dark corner, and another was on a sunny porch, the sun, rather than the plant food, may have been the reason for the plant's growth.

If it is difficult to determine all the possible causal factors for a fairly straightforward science experiment, imagine how difficult it is to determine the causal factors for things such as crime in America, violence in schools, cancer in middle-aged women, or strong reading habits in elementary children. If you can imagine all of the different factors that can influence these effects, you will begin to see that determining a single factor that brings about each of these effects can be very hard, and sometimes even impossible.

As humans, we like to find simple, single causes for things because it makes us feel more in control, and it reinforces our cherished beliefs (idols) about ourselves and the world. For example, if we can determine a single cause for an illness, then we feel more in control because we can avoid that cause and feel certain that we will not get the illness. Many fad diets are based on this concept of simple (and false) causal connections. Most researchers believe that being healthy requires a combination of good attitudes, positive behaviors, and good eating and exercise habits. Fad diets, on the other hand, tend to make claims that if people will eat a certain group of foods, or avoid eating a certain group of foods, then they will become really healthy. Sometimes there is some truth behind these claims, but usually the factors that make us healthy are much more complex than eating or not eating a certain food.

Another example that illustrates our love of simple, causal effects is some of the superstitions athletes have. For instance, you may be aware that many professional athletes have special items that they believe help them to hit homeruns or score winning touchdowns. For example, some

SEE, THE WAY I FIGURE IT, I GOT A B+ ON TODAY'S QUIZ AND I HARDLY STUDIED, SO JUST IMAGINE HOW WELL I'LL DO ON THE TEST IF I DON'T STUDY AT ALL.

athletes have been known to wear the same pair of socks or the same shirt to every game, without washing the clothing items, because the last three times they wore the socks or shirt, their team won. They believe the clothing item brings them success, somewhat like a lucky rabbit's foot. Similarly, some baseball pitchers do a certain action every time they pitch, such as scratching their ear or tapping their left toe three times on the ground. They believe that this action brings them good luck in their game. In all of these instances, these athletes are making faulty causal connections, but they hold on to their beliefs because they believe it will help their team win.

All of these examples illustrate a common fallacy called "false cause," which is also known in Latin as *post hoc ergo propter hoc* (literally, "After this, therefore, because of this"). This is a fallacy of weak induction. When people commit the fallacy of false cause, or *post hoc*, they argue that because A happened before B, A caused B. Referring back to our athlete example, the athlete reasons, "Because I wore these socks and my team won the game, the socks helped my team to win."

If we look at this fallacy in reference to the curfew debate, it is important to note that no curfew rule is the direct cause of a teenager's responsibility or irresponsibility. It can be one factor that influences his or her responsibility, but there are also many other factors that influence a teenager's behavior. Therefore, it is important, if you are trying to argue to your parents that a strict curfew could encourage irresponsibility and that a more lenient curfew could encourage responsibility, that you admit that this is only one possible cause of this result. Otherwise, you may be committing false cause.

Another closely related relationship fallacy is the fallacy of slippery slope, which, like false cause, is a fallacy of weak induction. When people commit slippery slope, they hypothesize that a certain cause will result in a disastrous chain of events, with little evidence to support that conclusion. For example, you would be committing this fallacy with the curfew debate if you argued with your parents in this way: "When parents impose curfews that are too strict, the stress and frustration builds and builds in their teenager until the teenager just explodes. Then, the teenager does something really desperate like stealing a car and going for a joy ride. Then the teenager will get pulled over for reckless driving, which will cause him to get grounded for an eternity from driving, which will cause more frustration. Finally, out of sheer desperation, the teenager will run away and end up homeless and destitute on the streets. This will cause the teen to fall into a life of crime, which will lead to long-term incarceration and years of hopeless despair, all because of the stupid curfew."

Of course, this argument is pure hyperbole (exaggeration), and it is unlikely that you would try to make an extreme argument like this with your parents. However, you still might try a less extreme form of slippery slope like this: "Parents who impose strict curfews cause stress and tension in their relationships with their children. This can cause years of unresolved conflict, which can ruin their relationships with their children and may even lead to the eventual severing of the relationship." This is a less extreme argument, but, if you notice, it still argues for a cause that sets off a disastrous chain of events, and, really, even though you may not like a strict curfew, there is no reason to believe that it will result in such dire consequences.

You may wonder how you can avoid the fallacies of false cause and slippery slope when using cause and effect as an argument technique. The best thing you can do is to realize, as mentioned earlier, that although some events or phenomena in life have a single cause, most have multiple causes. Therefore, avoid jumping to hasty conclusions and take the time to research other factors that may be causing an effect.

DEFINE

1. False Cause: ______________________________

2. *Post Hoc Ergo Propter Hoc*: ______________________________

3. Slippery Slope: ______________________________

EXPLAIN

Examples of Fallacies: Read each of the provided examples of fallacies, determine which fallacy has occurred, and explain why the premises of each example do not lead to the conclusion. Note: Some of the examples may be fallacies from previous chapters.

1. We cannot allow immigrants to continue entering our nation. If they do, the next thing we know, all people of English descent will be run out of the country, and we will have no place to live. We will be forced to live in the deserts or in the frozen regions like Antarctica, and then we will all die from exposure.

2. The South had a right to secede from the Union. It is like a student who must choose which class to take, and he can either take math or English. Either way, he knows he is going to have a lot of homework.

3. This is really weird! I am certain that my tennis shoes are giving me a headache. I wore them last Monday and then today, and both days I had a headache.

4. Congress wants to pass tighter gun control laws. Next thing you know, they will want to take away our hunting knives and crossbows, too, and pretty soon, all recreational weapons will be completely illegal.

EXPLAIN

5. We must not use violence against others to obtain our goals. Using violence against someone is like chasing an ice cream truck to get ice cream. You can chase the truck, but the driver will probably speed up, and you will get a terrible ache in your side from chasing the truck for so long.

6. A commercial slogan reads: "Olympus Distilled Water: The beverage of the gods!"

7. We need to go to the new Italian restaurant in town. My teacher, who has her Ph.D. in comparative literature, said it has the best Italian food she has ever tasted!

8. A little boy says to his mom, "Grandpa said that the new mayor is a rat. I didn't know animals could be in charge of cities!"

You have studied the common topics of definition, testimony, comparison, and relationship and have seen how they can help you build an effective argument. As a continued review of the common topics, read the following essay and answer the questions that follow.

Doctor's New Orders: Laugh a Little and Call Me in the Morning

Someone once said that laughter is the shortest distance between two people. This is certainly true, but many people don't realize that laughter accomplishes a multitude of other good things, as well, including resolving conflict, improving one's outlook on life, and increasing one's health and sense of well-being. These various positive results of laughter make it a priceless commodity.

In order to fully understand the benefits of laughter, it is important to understand what laughter is. To laugh is "to find amusement or pleasure in something, which leads to a verbalization of that amusement."[1] However, this definition does not fully reveal the true nature of laughter. In fact, there are actually two types of laughter. One type is negative laughter, which is when someone engages in demeaning, or hurtful, laughter. When someone laughs in this way, that person ridicules another. This type of laughter is destructive. The second type of laughter is positive laughter in which one finds joyful, rather than scornful, amusement in the craziness of life.

Some people may not understand the value of laughter, but it can be very beneficial. Interestingly, some health research has indicated that frequent laughter can help cure some diseases or send them into remission. In addition, laughter often helps to diffuse tension. Next time you are involved in an unpleasant argument, make a joke about yourself that makes the other person laugh and watch how it can improve the situation. Laughing frequently and consistently, every day, can help transform a negative person into a positive one. When one is constantly looking for and finding the absurd and hilarious in life, it is difficult to be gloomy.

Considering all the positive benefits of laughter, one might wonder why people do not laugh more often. People often become too busy, "sophisticated," or serious to be silly and carefree, both of which are attitudes that often generate laughter. Just watch young children laugh as they twirl around in circles, roll down hills, or chase bubbles and you'll see how being silly and carefree can make you laugh. Tragically, as we grow up, we often avoid these activities in order to appear more mature. Although adults cannot roll down every hill they see or chase bubbles at work all day, they can often do playful things at home, away from the ever-present public eye. At the very least, one can watch funny movies on a regular basis.

Laughter lightens; laughter energizes; laughter exhilarates. In fact, laughter might just be what the doctor ordered.

—Shelly Johnson

ANSWER

1. State the thesis of this essay in your own words. ______________________________

2. Find an example in the essay of each of the following common topics: definition, testimony, comparison, and relationship.

3. Identify one subtopic of the common topics that has not been used in this essay, and write three to five sentences that use that subtopic to develop this essay further. For example, you could use another definition or comparison technique.

FOLLOW UP

The common topics can be valuable for developing a wide array of persuasive topics. You can use them to persuade people to do things like adopt the use of a school uniform or a more lenient curfew, as with the arguments you have been developing as you go through this book. You can also use them to persuade people about an abstract or philosophical topic, as you did when you examined justice or your relationship with God.

For this exercise, choose an abstract or practical topic you wish to write about. To choose a topic, think about things that you care about a great deal or that interest you. For practical topics, you might explore the benefits of reading, the importance of friendship, or the dangers of sleep deprivation. For philosophical subjects, you could examine love, hate, envy, or beauty. Choose one of these to write about or choose another topic that interests you. Develop a thesis statement, gather persuasive evidence from all of the common topics you have explored so far and write an essay about your chosen topic.

COMMON TOPIC 5

Circumstance

Have you ever longed to do something, but someone told you it was impossible to do? Maybe you decided that you wanted to run a marathon, and when you told your best friend, he laughed at you and told you it was impossible. This may have discouraged you at first, but then you thought of several other long races that you ran. You realized that to run those races, you had to be disciplined, train hard, monitor your nutrition intake, and set incremental goals to help you achieve your final goal of running the race. After making that determination, you decide that the marathon is the same kind of thing, only on a larger scale. This kind of thinking illustrates the common topic of circumstance.

Under the common topic of circumstance are the subtopics **possible and impossible** and **past and future fact**.

Possible and Impossible: This subtopic examines why something can or cannot occur or be done.

Past and Future Fact: This subtopic examines what has happened in the past and what this means for present circumstances.

As you may have recognized, this topic often requires you to examine history to determine what might happen in the future. You have probably heard the old saying that those who ignore the errors of history are doomed to repeat them. This common topic makes good use of the wisdom behind that statement.

In the movie *The Pursuit of Happyness*, actor Will Smith plays a man named Chris Gardner, who experienced hard times in his life. His job wasn't going well, and he was struggling to provide for the basic needs of his wife and young son. His landlord was threatening to evict him, and Gardner was very discouraged. One day, when things were looking really bad, Chris met a stockbroker, and Chris decided that he wanted to become a stockbroker because he knew he could do it. He knew he would be able to provide for his family with the money he would make as a stockbroker. Many people told him that it was impossible, but he believed that he could do it, and eventually he succeeded.

Chris seemed to have several different beliefs that motivated him. He knew that other people had hard times, but that they pulled through. He knew that he had had better times in the past, and that his life could get better again. He knew that people like him had achieved great things with hard work, intelligence, and commitment. He knew that he had all of those traits, so he knew that he could achieve great things, too. He also believed that he had already achieved harder things, including surviving the end of his marriage and loving and taking care of his young son, even when they were evicted from their apartment and had to spend the night locked in the bathroom of a subway restroom and sleep on the floor.

He probably didn't realize it, but one thing that helped Chris Gardner convince himself he could achieve his dreams was the subtopic of possible and impossible. There are several different ways this subtopic can be used:

1. If one of a pair of similar things is possible, the other is, too.[1] For example, in some high schools, students are required to write a senior thesis, which is an involved project that takes significant research, writing, and presentation skills. These students may also be required to write a similar paper during their senior year in college. If a student was nervous about writing his college senior thesis, he could reason that because the two papers are similar, and he was able to accomplish his high school thesis, he can therefore succeed in writing his college thesis.

2. If the more difficult of two things is possible, then the easier is possible, too.[2] To illustrate this, let us imagine that a girl loves backpacking and, in fact, has taken a class that required her to survive on her own for a week in the woods. This was a very difficult task—she had to find and cook her own food, set up her shelter, and constantly keep her bearings and sense of direction in unfamiliar territory. Later, when she is on a backpacking trip with friends, they temporarily get lost. Although she panics a little at first, she realizes that since she survived her week in the woods on her own, which was much harder, she can handle this small crisis.

3. If something can have a beginning, it can have an end, and if something can have an end, it can have a beginning.[3] When I was growing up and became discouraged about something in my life, my mom would always tell me "This too shall pass." Without realizing it, Mom was using the subtopic of possible and impossible to cheer me up. She reasoned that if bad times could begin, they could also end. Similarly, you could reason that if good times have an end, they can also begin again. By reasoning this way, you are using the method of developing the sub-topic of possible and impossible.

4. If the parts of a thing are possible, then the whole is possible; and conversely, if the whole is possible, the parts are possible.[4] At one time or another in our lives, most of us have had to work on a really big project that, when viewed as a whole, seemed really overwhelming. It might have been a re search paper, a science project, or, for some of us, cleaning the disaster area that is our room. Rather than thinking about these projects as a crushing, overwhelming whole, it is often better to break them down into smaller steps. When you do this, you suddenly realize that you can do each of the little steps, and therefore, the whole project is not as hard as it originally seemed. If you reason this way, you are determining that because the parts of something are possible, the whole is possible.

If the parts of a thing are possible, then the whole is possible

5. If a thing can be produced without art or preparation, it certainly can be done with the help of art or planning.[5] When I was in college, I took a creative writing class in which I was required to write a story. I remember feeling extremely nervous about this. I might have relieved some of my stress if I had considered the fact that I had written a thirty-page novelette one summer in high school. I just got an interesting idea in my mind and started writing. The next thing I knew, I had written a thirty-page story. Had I considered this, I might have realized that if I could write a story without any preparation or instruction, I could certainly do it when I had a teacher guiding and teaching me through the process.

To further clarify this subtopic, let's relate it to the example of the marathon provided in the introduction to the common topic of circumstance. The numbers in parentheses correspond with the list of different ways you can argue using the subtopic of possible and impossible. Your friend believes it's impossible for you to run a marathon, but you believe it's possible. How do you know? You reason that you have run other races that were lengthy and on a similar terrain. You reason that if you could succeed in those other races, you could run the marathon (1). You also know that many people your age have run marathons, so you reason that if they can do it, you can do it, too. You have also heard that breaking the ten-mile barrier is much harder, mentally, than running a marathon, and since you have already run ten miles several times, you believe that you have already achieved the difficult part (2).

You might also reason that marathons don't go on forever. They begin, and a few hours later they end. You know that remembering this fact always gets you through races when the running gets really difficult and strenuous (3). You also know that running a marathon takes discipline, endurance, practice, and patience, and you believe you have all of those skills. Therefore, you believe you can run the marathon (4). Lastly, you know that you have loved running ever since you were little, and there were times that you just went out and ran three or four miles,

YA KNOW, BRENDA, I FEEL LIKE IF I CAN HANDLE BABYSITTING THESE TWO, MAYBE I SHOULD TRY LOOKING FOR A JOB AS A STUNT-WOMAN OR NAVY SEAL.

without even training. You decide that if you can get this far without training, you can get much farther with training (5). As you argued with yourself about whether or not you could run a marathon, you used all of the possible ways to develop the subtopic of possible and impossible. As you can see, fully exploring this topic can help you to construct a strong argument.

Let's apply this subtopic to your curfew argument. You know that even though your parents generally trust you, they are a little bit nervous about whether you will use the privilege of a more lenient curfew responsibly. You realize that this is a perfect opportunity for you to use the subtopic of possible and impossible. You could argue this way: First, you remind your parents of the time when they went on a retreat for a week, and you stayed at home with your brother and managed the house. You remind them that you were very responsible during that time. You kept the house clean, fixed meals for your brother, and you did not have any wild parties. You reason with your parents that if you were responsible for a whole week when you had total freedom, you can be responsible with the limited freedom of your weekend curfew.

Next, you reason with your parents that you have already proven your responsibility in a much harder situation. You have maintained a high grade point average all through junior high and your first two years of high school. And, you point out, you maintained this even when your parents stopped checking your homework regularly and making sure that you were studying for tests. You further explain to your parents that you know that in order to use a more lenient curfew responsibly, there are several important things you need to do. You must respect your parents' authority, you must demonstrate an awareness of possible dangers that you could run into when driving at night, you must be wise and mature enough to stay out of dangerous situations, and you must demonstrate care for your personal safety and the safety of others.

You explain to your parents that you have considered all of these things, and you list some examples of times when you have done them. Lastly, you point out to your parents that you are naturally an obedient, respectful, and thoughtful child. That is, you practice responsibility even when you aren't thinking about it. You reason with your parents that if you show these character traits when you *aren't* thinking about it, you can show them even more when you *are* thinking about it. You make your argument eloquently, and, at last, you have the suspicion that your parents are starting to soften.

EXPLAIN

1. List several different ways in which you could develop an argument using the topic of possible and impossible. For instance, the first idea mentioned about this subtopic was "If one of a pair of similar things is possible, the other is, too."

IDENTIFY

Arguments from Possible and Impossible: Read the provided famous arguments that use the subtopic of possible and impossible. Then, identify the argument from possible and impossible used by the authors.

1. From the "Death of Socrates"

But neither did I then think that I ought, for the sake of avoiding danger, to do anything unworthy of a freeman, nor do I now repent of having so defended myself; but I should much rather choose to die having so defended myself than to live in that way. For neither in a trail nor in battle is it right that I or anyone else should employ every possible means whereby he may avoid death; for in battle it is frequently evident that a man might escape death by laying down his arms and throwing himself on the mercy of his pursuers. And there are many other devices in every danger, by which to avoid death, if a man dares to do and say everything. But this is not difficult, O Athenians, to escape death, but it is much more difficult to avoid depravity, for it runs swifter than death. And now I, being slow and aged, am overtaken by the slower of the two; But my accusers, being strong and active, have been overtaken by the swifter, wickedness. And now I depart, condemned by you to death; but they condemned by truth, as guilty of iniquity and injustice: and I abide my sentence and so do they.[6]

IDENTIFY

2. Caitline to the Conspirators

But success (I call gods and men to witness!) is in our own hands. Our years are fresh, our spirit is unbroken; among our oppressors, on the contrary, through age and wealth a general debility has been produced. We have, therefore, only to make a beginning; the course of events will accomplish the rest.[7]

IDENTIFY

3. John Wesley's "God's Love to Fallen Man"

What are termed afflictions in the language of men are in the language of God styled blessings. Indeed, had there been no suffering in the world, a considerable part of religion, yea, and in some respects, the most excellent part, could have had no place therein: since the very existence of it depends on our suffering: so that had there been no pain it could have had no being. Upon this foundation, even our suffering, it is evident all our passive graces are built; yea, the noblest of all Christian graces, love enduring all things.[8]

IDENTIFY

4. From Thomas Aquinas' "An Argument for the Existence of God from Beginning and End"

We find in nature things that are possible to be and not to be, since they are found to be generated, and to be corrupted, and consequently they are possible to be and not to be. But it is impossible for these always to exist, for that which is possible not to be at some time is not. Therefore, if everything is possible not to be, then at one time there could be nothing in existence. Now if this were true, even now there would be nothing in existence, because that which does not exist only begins to exist by something already existing. Therefore, if at one time nothing was in existence, it would have been impossible for anything to have begun to exist. And thus even now nothing would be in existence, which is clearly false. Therefore, not all beings are merely possible, but there must exist something the existence of which is necessary. But every necessary thing either has its necessity caused by another or not. Now it is impossible to go on to infinity in necessary things which have their necessity caused by another, as been already proved in regard to efficient causes. Therefore, we must admit the existence of some being having of itself its own necessity, and not receiving it from another, buy rather causing in others their necessity. This all men speak of as God.[9]

IDENTIFY

5. John Ruskin's "On Managing Riches"

There is assuredly no action of our social life, however unimportant, which, by kindly thought, may not be made to have a beneficial influence upon others; and it is impossible to spend the smallest sum of money, for any not absolutely necessary purpose, without a grave responsibility attaching to the manner of spending it. The object we ourselves covet may, indeed, be desirable and harmless, so far as we are concerned, but the providing us with it may, perhaps, be a very prejudicial occupation to someone else. And then it becomes instantly a moral question, whether we are to indulge ourselves or not. Whatever we wish to buy, we ought first to consider not only if the thing be fit for us, but if the manufacture of it be a wholesome and happy one.[10]

BRAINSTORM

Dress Code and Arguments from Possible and Impossible: Now that you are more familiar with arguments from possible and impossible, brainstorm some arguments with this common topic that support your thesis statement for the uniform debate. Write a paragraph containing at least one argument from possible and impossible. Use the provided questions to help you get started.

1. What is something similar to uniforms that has a positive or negative effect on school atmosphere? How does this show that it is possible for uniforms to have a positive or negative effect on school atmosphere?

2. What praiseworthy goal are you trying to accomplish through adopting uniforms or discouraging their adoption? Think of a goal or a purpose similar to this that has already been achieved. How can you use this example to support your thesis?

3. Which of the other development strategies for possible and impossible could you use to develop your thesis?

CHAPTER 21 *Subtopic: Past and Future Fact*

When you use the subtopic of past and future fact, you examine what has happened in the past in order to draw conclusions about what is likely to happen in the present. If you have ever listened to a politician give a speech, you have likely heard him use this subtopic. When politicians run for office, especially the office of president, they often argue that they will do a good job now because they have done a good job in the past. For example, many men who have been elected president of the United States served in the military. Often they will tell of hardships they have endured in the military, horrible battles they have survived, honors they have won, and difficult missions they have carried out. Before John F. Kennedy became president, he was in the US Navy during World War II. At one point in that war, a boat that Kennedy was on with several other Navy officers was hit and destroyed by enemy fire. Kennedy and his crewmates abandoned ship, and were floating in the ocean. One of the crew had been severely wounded by the blast. Kennedy grabbed hold of this crewmate and swam to shore, which was quite a distance away, saving the man's life.[1] When Kennedy was running for president, his supporters often told stories like this to demonstrate Kennedy's bravery, fortitude, and presence of mind in difficult situations. Politicians tell these stories because they want to prove that if they have done difficult things in the past, they can do difficult things in the present and in the future. If they have shown bravery and wisdom in life-threatening situations in the past, they can do it in the present and in the future.

Just as with the subtopic of possible and impossible, there are several different ways that you can develop the subtopic of past and future fact.

1. If the less probable of two events has occurred, the more probable event is likely to have occurred, too.[2] For example, let's say that you have a friend who has been your best friend for years. Then, sadly, you have an argument and you are no longer friends. Shortly thereafter, another friend reveals to you that your best friend has revealed some of your most personal secrets. You can't believe it. Before the fight, you would never have believed that your friend would even think bad things about you much less betray your trust. However, you discover that, indeed, this friend is committing the ultimate betrayal and sharing your secrets with others. Then, another friend tells you that your best friend is also saying bad things about you behind your back. Once this has been revealed, you have no trouble believing it because you already know that she is telling your secrets.

2. If something that naturally follows something else has occurred, then that something else [the antecedent] has happened, too; and conversely, if the antecedents were present, then the natural consequences occurred, too.[3] If you are like many children, you look forward to the occasional snow day during the winter. From your great longing for snow days, you have probably figured out that

snow usually comes from a combination of rain and low temperatures. Therefore, when snow is predicted and it is cold and raining outside, you probably become much more hopeful than if the temperatures are warmer and it is not raining. When you reason this way, you are examining the past to determine what consequences follow particular antecedents.

3. If someone had the power and the desire and the opportunity to do something, he or she has done it.[4] Policemen often think in this manner when they are trying to determine who is the most likely suspect in a crime. For instance, imagine that someone has broken into a bike shop and stolen several expensive bikes. The police will likely check first on the people who work in the bike store. Is this because people who work in bike stores tend to be criminals? Certainly not. It is because it is often the case that if someone has the power, desire, and opportunity to do something, he or she has done it. There are a number of factors that support this line of thinking in the case of the stolen bikes. For instance, the people who work in the bike store probably like bikes a lot, so they would have an incentive to steal the bikes. They also have more power and opportunity to steal the bikes than people who do not work in the store because they know the schedule of the store, as well as possible weak points in the store's security system. The police might further investigate some of the store employees who seem to have a greater motive to steal than others. For instance, the police may try to find someone who is in desperate need of money. This person might be a more likely suspect because he would have a greater motive for stealing the bikes: so he could sell them and make money quickly. In addition, the police would also probably look for an employee who has greater opportunity than other employees, such as the person who locks the store up at night, or who knows a lot about the security system. As you can see, reasoning in such a way could help the police narrow their possibilities and build a strong case.

4. If the antecedents of something are present, then the natural consequences will occur.[5] When you are faced with a hard task that you fear you cannot accomplish, this argument strategy can help you convince yourself that you can do it. For instance, if you desire to get good grades at school, but fear you cannot do it, it may help you to consider what getting good grades requires. The antecedents of good grades are knowledge of class material, usually some intelligence, attention in class, good organization and study habits, and perseverance. It is very unusual for someone to have all or most of these characteristics and yet do poorly in school. We can say that good grades are a natural consequence of these antecedents. Therefore, if a student desires good grades, he should make sure that these antecedents are present in his life.

You can use the subtopics of antecedent and consequence and possible and impossible to develop a past and future fact argument.

As you were reading through this list, you may have noticed that while the subtopic of past and future fact is different than the subtopics of antecedent and consequence and possible and impossible, you can use those subtopics to develop a past and future fact argument.

By now, you may be thinking about your curfew debate whenever you learn more about the common topics and their subtopics. You may be able to see how you could use these development strategies to argue for a more lenient curfew. You could go back to the example mentioned in chapter 20 of the time your parents went away on a retreat for a week and you stayed at home and took care of your younger brother. You could argue that if you were going to be irresponsible and freak out, you would have done it during that week. Since you were extremely responsible during that week, you argue that it is very reasonable that you will be responsible with a more lenient curfew.

You could also argue that the antecedents of responsibility are good morals, formed by strong boundaries and good discipline when a child is young. You could emphasize to your parents that you had good boundaries and discipline when you were younger, and you have demonstrated the good morals that come from having that background. Therefore, you could argue that, since all of the antecedents for responsibility are in place, responsibility will certainly follow. You could also argue that if someone has the power, desire and opportunity to do something, they will. You can demonstrate that you certainly have the desire, power, and opportunity to be responsible, and you can point out that a more lenient curfew will allow you to prove this.

At this point, your parents may be so impressed with your careful and well-reasoned argument that they will accept your proposal.

ANSWER

1. 1. List several different ways in which you could develop an argument using the subtopic of past and future fact. For instance, the second idea mentioned about this subtopic was: "If something that naturally follows something else has occurred, then that something else [the antecedent] has happened, too; and conversely, if the antecedents were present, then the natural consequences occurred, too."

ANALYZE

Arguments from Past and Future Fact: For each of the provided excerpts, determine the thesis of the argument. Then, determine the argument from past and future fact that the authors use.

1. Patrick Henry's "Give Me Liberty or Give Me Death"

Let us not, I beseech you, sir, deceive ourselves longer. Sir, we have done everything that could be done, to avert the storm which is now coming on. We have petitioned; we have remonstrated; we have supplicated; we have prostrated ourselves before the throne, and have implored its interposition to arrest the tyrannical hands of the ministry and parliament. Our petitions have been slighted; our remonstrances have produced additional violence and insult; our supplications have been disregarded; and we have been spurned, with contempt, from the foot of the throne. In vain, after these things may we indulge the fond hope of peace and reconciliation.[6]

ANALYZE

2. Augustine's Chap. 40: "Whatever has been rightly said by the heathen, we must appropriate to our uses."

Moreover, if those who are called philosophers, and especially the Platonists, have said aught that is true and in harmony with our faith, we are not only not to shrink from it, but to claim it for our own use from those who have unlawful possession of it. For as the Egyptians had not only the idols and heavy burdens which the people of Israel hated and fled from, but also vessels and ornaments of gold and silver, and garments, which the same people when going out of Egypt appropriated to themselves designing them for a better use, not doing this on their own authority, but by the command of God, the Egyptians themselves, in their ignorance, providing them with things which they themselves were not making good use of; in the same way, all branches of heathen learning have not only false and superstitious fancies and heavy burdens of unnecessary toil, which every one of us, when going out under the leadership of Christ from the fellowship of the heathen, ought to abhor and avoid; but they contain also liberal instruction which is better adapted to the use of the truth, and some most excellent precepts of morality; and some truths in regard even to the worship of the One God are found among them. Now these are, so to speak, their gold and silver, which they did not create themselves, but dug out of the mines of God's providence which are everywhere scattered abroad, and are perversely and unlawfully prostituting to the worship of devils. These, therefore, the Christian, when he separates himself in spirit from the miserable fellowship of these men, ought to take away from them, and to devote to their proper use in preaching the gospel.[7]

EXAMINE

Dress Code and Arguments from Past and Future Fact: Examine the different strategies you can use for developing arguments from past and future fact. Which ones will work for supporting your thesis about dress code? Select several and develop a paragraph using them.

CHAPTER 22 *Fallacies of Circumstance*

There are several fallacies commonly committed when using the common topic of circumstance in an argument. First, let's revisit a fallacy we discussed when we were looking at the common topic of comparison: false analogy. You may remember that when you use the subtopics of possible and impossible or past and future fact, it is very common to look at events that have occurred in the past in order to make comparisons to the present. When you compare a past and a present event and draw a conclusion from this comparison, you are using a type of analogy. Therefore, it is important that you avoid constructing false analogies when developing an argument using those subtopics.

When you commit the fallacy of false analogy, you base a conclusion on a comparison of two items that are so dissimilar that no conclusion should be drawn. For example, a student who dislikes school uniforms might argue, "Students should be able to choose whatever clothes they want to wear to school. After all, when people go to purchase a car, they can choose whatever car they want." At first, it may seem like this comparison has some merit, but as you think about the two items being compared—clothes that you wear to school and a car that is being purchased—it becomes apparent that these items are too dissimilar to warrant any conclusion. For instance, one of the reasons many schools adopt a student dress code is because they feel that some of the styles, colors, or types of outfits that students might choose on their own would be distracting to their fellow classmates. The same thing could not be said regarding the style, color, or type of car that someone might choose because it is highly unlikely that any of those features would be distracting to any dangerous or significant degree to another driver. Therefore, because of the dissimilarities between school uniforms and cars, it is not proper to draw a conclusion from their comparison. It is a weak, or false, analogy.

Now that you have reviewed this fallacy, it needs to be examined in a slightly different light in order to determine how someone might commit it with the common topic of circumstance. To understand the fallacy of false analogy in light of this topic, think back to the example of running a marathon discussed in chapter 20, which covered the subtopic of possible and impossible. In the example, you supported your plan for running a marathon by arguing that you had run similar, although shorter, races (like a ten-mile race). Since you were successful in running that race, you reasoned that you could train to run the longer distance of a marathon. At first, this seems like a near-perfect comparison. After all, the training for running a marathon is very similar to what you would do for running a ten-mile race, it just takes more time. Therefore, if you had the patience and time to train for the ten–mile race, it seems to make sense that you could train for the marathon.

However, these situations may not be as similar as they first appear. For example, you may have run the ten-mile race five years ago, and after the race, you had a skiing accident and broke your leg. In addition, the marathon that you want to run is in Denver, Colorado, which is at a significantly higher altitude than the city in which you ran your ten-mile race. Running at a higher altitude makes

a race significantly more difficult. Although you may still be able to run the race, it is important to consider these factors because it may be that your analogy between the marathon and the ten-mile race is a false one. Are the two races somewhat similar? Certainly. However, the two factors we mentioned—a broken leg and the change in altitude—make the two races less similar than if you had never broken your leg and you were running the marathon in the same city in which you ran the ten-mile race.

Let's look at the fallacy of false analogy in light of your curfew argument. You might remember that one of the arguments you constructed to present to your parents was that since you had been responsible in other situations requiring great maturity, such as when your parents left for the week and you had to manage the house and watch your little brother. you will also be responsible with a more lenient curfew, which also requires maturity. This may be a very effective argument, and you could certainly argue that there are some similarities between the two situations. However, there may be some differences you have not considered. For instance, although your parents did, indeed, trust you all alone for a whole week, that was a one-time situation with very strict parameters. It is different from a weekend curfew that requires you to make good decisions every week.

In addition, when your parents left you on your own, you were still in a highly controlled situation with clear boundaries. You were in your house, and you were carrying out set routines, which had been established by your parents. With a curfew, you are not in your house, and a whole new set of variables emerge. When you leave your house, factors such as friends, traffic conditions, and other drivers who may or may not be responsible and well-intentioned will affect you. As you can see from these examples, the short time when your parents left you in charge of the house and the time that would be affected by a more lenient curfew are not completely identical.

At this point, I want to remind you of something I mentioned before: no analogy is perfect. Whenever you are comparing two items, the comparison will eventually break down. The goal, then, is to draw conclusions from two items that are so similar that at least some comparison and conclusion is warranted. In the paragraph above, it is true that the two instances being compared are not identical. However, both do require wisdom, impulse control, follow-through, and adherence to previously established guidelines. Therefore, it is still acceptable to make a comparison between the two situations. It is wise, however, to admit the limitations of the comparison. If you don't, your opponent, which in this case would be your parents, likely will. Admitting the weaknesses of a comparison from the beginning can actually strengthen your position, as long as you can demonstrate why the dissimilarities between the two items in your analogy are not of major concern.

Keep the example of the time that your parents left you at home for a week in mind as you consider another common fallacy. You might recall that one of the ways you can develop the subtopic of past and future fact is to use an argument from antecedent and consequence. An argument from antecedent and consequence is structured something like this:

"If A, then B,"

"A; therefore B."

The "if A" part is the antecedent, and the "then B" part is the consequence. This argument works by stating that if a certain factor, A, is present, then a certain outcome, B, will also be present. The argument then affirms that factor A is, indeed, present; therefore B must also be present. For instance, you might argue, "If there is a foot of snow on the ground, then school will be canceled. There is a foot of snow on the ground; therefore, school will be canceled." In this argument, "a foot of snow on the ground" is the antecedent, and "school will be canceled" is the consequence.

You might remember that in your argument for a more lenient curfew, you noted that the antecedents of responsibility are strong boundaries set by parents when a child is young, and loving but consistent discipline. You argued that because you had strong boundaries and consistent and loving discipline, you would certainly act responsibly with a more lenient curfew. In this argument, "strong boundaries and loving but consistent discipline" were your antecedents, and "responsibility" was your consequence.

This kind of argument can be very effective; however, as you construct an argument from antecedent and consequence, you must avoid committing two fallacies. The first fallacy is the fallacy of **denying the antecedents**. When someone denies the antecedents, he argues, "If A, then B. Not A; therefore not B." At first, this may seem logical, but if the "A" and "B" in this argument are replaced with real-life situations, the fallacy will become clear. For example, let's say someone argued, "If someone is kind and friendly, she will have friends. Sue is not kind or friendly. Therefore, she does not have friends." You have probably already figured out the problem with this. Although being kind and friendly is one of the best ways to gain friends, people who do not have these traits can also make friends. It may be that a person is very shy, and so they don't seem kind or friendly at first; however, over time, that person proves himself loyal and supportive. Therefore, he has friends. Furthermore, sometimes people build friendships on a foundation of mutual negativity, rudeness, meanness, and an ability to insult others. Of course, some of us might not consider this a true friendship, but nevertheless, such "friendships" do exist. The point is, just because a certain antecedent is not present doesn't mean that the outcome is not present either. There might be other antecedents that lead to this outcome.

If we look at this in light of the curfew debate, you would commit this fallacy if you argued, "If a teenager is wild, reckless, and drunk, he will have a car accident. I am not wild, reckless, or drunk. Therefore, I will not have a car accident." Car accidents can occur because of other factors besides wildness, recklessness, and drunkenness. Therefore, when you argue, "If A, then B", you can affirm that "A" is true, and, therefore, "B" is also true. But, you cannot argue that because "A" is not true, "B" is not true.

The second fallacy someone can commit with an antecedent and consequence argument is the fallacy of **affirming the consequence**. This occurs when someone argues, "If A, then B. B, therefore A ." In regard to your curfew, you would commit this fallacy if you argued, "If a teenager is truthful, he will have a good relationship with his parents. I have a good relationship with my parents; therefore I am truthful." As you can see, this argument does not work. There are many teenagers who have good relationships with their parents, but the teenagers are not always truthful. It may be that the parents, unfortunately, don't care if their child is dishonest. Or, it may be that they haven't found out about the dishonesty yet, and so their relationship is built on a sense of false security. You would probably craft an argument like this because you are, indeed, honest and you want to emphasize this to your parents. Honesty is a good thing to emphasize; however, the previous argument would not be a good one to use in order to emphasize it.

At this point, you have a strong supply of good argument strategies, and you also know which mistakes you should avoid while constructing your arguments. In the next chapter, we will look at several general fallacies that, while they do not pertain to any certain common topic, are still commonly committed fallacies.

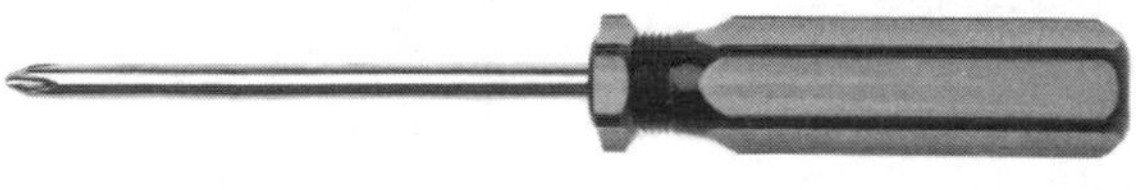

ANSWER

1. What must you pay particular attention to if you want to avoid the fallacy of false analogy when you are comparing a current situation to a past situation? ______________________________

2. What is the basic structure of an argument from antecedent and consequence? ______________________________

3. What is the fallacy of denying the antecedent? ______________________________

4. What is the fallacy of affirming the consequence? ______________________________

EXPLAIN

Examining Arguments: For each of the provided arguments, explain what fallacy is being committed and why the argument is fallacious.

1. If students are able to express their personalities by choosing their own school clothes, they will be happy. The students in this school cannot express their personalities by choosing their own clothes. Therefore, they will not be happy.

____

2. I don't think that my school should adopt uniforms. When I was in junior high, my parents sent me to a military school for kids with behavioral problems. We had to wear uniforms there, and all of those kids had terrible attitudes. Therefore, if my school adopts uniforms, I know all of the students will have bad attitudes.

____

EXPLAIN

3. If students are able to choose what they wear to school, they will be happy. These students are happy. Therefore, they must be able to choose what they will wear to school.

4. If a school requires its students to wear a school uniform, there will be order in the school. This school is orderly. Therefore, it must require school uniforms.

5. If a school requires its students to wear a school uniform, there will be order in the school. This school does not require students to wear a school uniform. Therefore, the school will not be orderly.

6. I think my junior high should have a uniform. When I was in kindergarten, the school I was in had a uniform, and all of the students were extremely well behaved. Therefore, I think that if my junior high would adopt a school uniform, the students would be much better behaved.

Now that you have studied all of the common topics, it is time to examine how they all work together. Read the following essay and then answer the questions that follow.

If You Wish to Have Friends, Be Friendly

Have you ever noticed that there are some people who always seem to be surrounded by friends? It seems like other people are just naturally attracted to them, and you wonder, "How do they do it?" Perhaps it has to do with their talents, or the fact that they are great athletes, or maybe they are really funny, or have an amazing intellect, or a really great sense of fashion. Although all of these attributes can attract people, the secret to friendship may surprise you. As Seneca, an ancient Roman orator (speaker), once said, "*Si vis amari, ama*," or, "If you wish to be loved, love."[1] In other words, if you wish to have friends, you must be friendly, and when you are friendly, you will have friends.

In order to understand the concept of friendliness, it may help to explore several common definitions of this term. Webster's dictionary defines the term "friendly" as "exhibiting good will and an absence of antagonism."[2] Also according to Webster, the word "friendliness" "stresses cordiality and often warmth or intimacy of personal relationships."[3] Two synonyms for the word "friendly" are "neighborly" and "amicable." Webster's states that the word "amicable" "implies a state of peace and a desire on the part of the parties not to quarrel," while the word "neighborly" "implies a disposition to live on good terms with others and be helpful on principle."[4] In contrast, several common antonyms of "friendly" are "hostile," "antagonistic," "rude," "cold," and "distant"—all words that imply a significantly *unfriendly* atmosphere. From these definitions and words, it becomes apparent that being friendly implies showing good will, warmth, and kindness to others, a desire to show an interest in other people's concerns, and a desire not to offend or hurt them. On the other hand, when someone is unfriendly, he often holds himself at a distance from others, as though he doesn't care about them and their interests, or, in more extreme situations, is hostile toward them, their interests, and beliefs.

When people are friendly to others, the most common signs of this are smiling, showing an interest in people, or inviting them to be a part of a group or to participate in events. Friendly people also often make small physical gestures that make people feel at ease, such as making eye contact, nodding while listening intently, or touching the arm of the person to whom they are talking or listening as a sign of empathy or compassion. They often compliment others, recognizing the best in them, and they may also do special things, such as remembering others' birthdays, writing them encouraging notes, or telling them jokes to cheer them up. In essence, friendly people are tuned in to other people's feelings and thoughts and do the best they can to create a positive, warm environment for other people.

An interesting historical example may add some further illumination to this concept. Mother Teresa was a nun who lived from 1910 to 1997. She became known for caring for the friendless and outcast of society, such as the lepers in India.[5] She took in people that others had left on the streets to die. She cleansed their wounds, fed them, and cured them. And, for those who were about to die, she was a warm, caring friend for them at the end of their lives.[6] She was known to say things like, "Loneliness and the feeling of being unwanted is the most terrible poverty," and "Every time you smile at someone, it is an action of love, a gift to that person, a beautiful thing."[7] Mother Teresa had no great talent except her amazing heart, but she was universally admired, respected, and loved because of the friendliness and love she showed to everyone.

When we examine the definition of friendliness and these examples, we realize that when we are friendly, we make it possible for people to feel warm, relaxed and appreciated. People like to be around others who make them feel this way. You could say that being friendly is like giving good news. If you observe carefully the next time someone shares good news with a group of people, you will notice that this automatically creates good will toward the bringer of the news. This is because we like to be around people who make us feel good. It is as though we associate our good feelings with the person, even if all the person is doing is relating some happy news to us. In the same way, when people are friendly, it creates good feelings in others, just like bearing good news, and people associate pleasant feelings with the friendly person and desire to be around that person.

On the other hand, when someone is hostile, cold, and distant to others, or when that person shows a lack of concern for others' interests and well-being, it makes it almost impossible for people to relax around that person. Coldness, hostility, or antagonism imply, at the least, a carelessness or lack of regard about others' well-being, and, in the worst cases, a desire to hurt or damage others in some way. It is impossible for us to relax around people like this, for we never know when they may actually hurt or betray us.

As you read about what it takes to gain friends, you may feel overwhelmed, especially if you are shy. However, it may help you to feel less intimidated if you break the process down into small steps. Start by listing what individual actions communicate friendliness. Some of the most common ones are smiling, making eye contact with people when you speak with them, and asking questions about them and their interests. Another gesture of friendliness is noticing the best in people and complimenting them on those things. To be friendly, you also need to invite people to be a part of your life in some way. For instance, you might ask them to come to your house for a get-together or

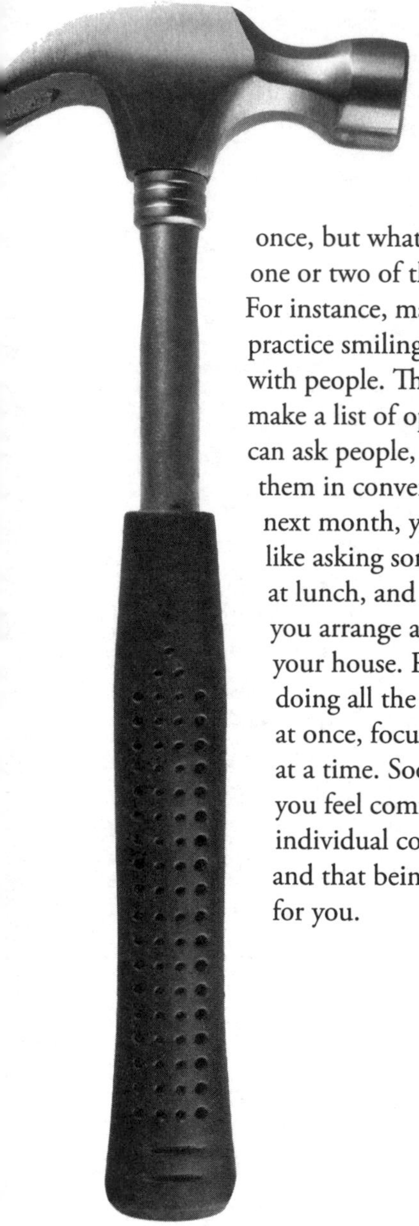

ask them to go to a fun event like a movie. It may seem overwhelming to do all of these things at once, but what if you only practiced one or two of these things each month? For instance, maybe the first month, you practice smiling and making eye contact with people. The next month, you make a list of open-ended questions you can ask people, and you practice using them in conversations. Maybe the next month, you try something small like asking someone to sit with you at lunch, and then the next month, you arrange a little get-together at your house. Rather than focusing on doing all the steps to being friendly at once, focus on doing them one at a time. Soon, you will realize that you feel comfortable doing all of the individual components of friendliness and that being friendly is very easy for you.

It may also help you to recognize that you likely already know how to do all or most of the components of friendliness because you have done all or most of them before at one time or another. Therefore, you have all the antecedents of friendliness, and once you start practicing them together, friendliness will naturally follow. Furthermore, it's also helpful to remember that you have probably had friends before in your life. You might feel like you haven't had many friends, but you've most likely at least had a few. Realize that when you made those friends, you weren't even thinking about being friendly—you just naturally made friends. If you can make friends when you aren't even trying, you can certainly make friends when you *are* trying.

Gaining friends is not a matter of having great intellect, riches, or brilliant talents. The simple truth is that people like to be around people who make them feel warm, appreciated, and accepted. The great news is that everyone has the power to make people feel that way. A whole world of friends is waiting for you if you have the desire to make them. Therefore, if you want to have friends, go and be friendly!

—Shelly Johnson

ANSWER

1. What is the thesis of this essay? ____

____

____

____

2. How is the common topic of circumstance used in this essay? ______________________

____

____

____

____

____

____

____

SURVEY

1. You will notice that the last part of this essay specifically uses the common topic of circumstance, including arguments from possible and impossible and past and future fact. You will recall that there are several strategies for developing possible and impossible and past and future fact. Find two of the strategies used in the last three paragraphs and write them in the space provided below.

____

____

____

2. Think of one other strategy for developing possible and impossible and past and future fact and explain how that strategy could have been developed to support the thesis of this essay.

____

____

____

____

____

____

3. In this essay, in addition to circumstance, I have used all of the other common topics—definition, relationship, comparison, and testimony. Locate and underline each of these common topics in the essay, writing in the margin which of thc topics it is.

The primary goal of this book has been to teach you how to build arguments, so you have only received a brief introduction to fallacies. There are many other fallacies that it is important for you to learn about so that you can avoid them as you build your arguments.

You might remember from the beginning of this that when people get very emotional (sad, angry, or happy) about a topic, it is easy for them to commit fallacies. This is because people desire to prove their conclusions so strongly that they focus on what they want rather than on whether or not what they want is right or good. In order to build solid arguments that are free from the pitfalls of being too emotionally involved in your subject, you must learn about some of the most common fallacies people commit when they get into an emotional state of mind. These fallacies are: ***ad hominem***, **appeal to pity**, and the **straw man fallacy**.

When people get very emotional about a topic, it is easy for them to commit fallacies.

The first fallacy is *ad hominem*, which is a Latin phrase meaning "at the man." This fallacy is committed when a person attacks the person with whom he or she is arguing rather than attacking the person's argument. For example, let us say that a man named Paul Smith was running for president. His opponent might argue, "Paul Smith claims that he will do what is right for our country, but what he does not tell you is that he was once arrested for drunk driving." On the surface, this argument seems persuasive. After all, we certainly do not want to have a drunkard or a lawbreaker as our president. However, how do we know these things are true about Paul Smith? What evidence does his accuser have? It could be that Paul Smith was once arrested for drunk driving when he was young; however, since then, he has reformed, and now he would make a wonderful president. Unless Paul Smith is currently a drunkard and lawbreaker, this argument is fallacious because the arguer is attacking Paul Smith about things irrelevant to Paul's current possible performance as president. People most often commit *ad hominem* when they don't like the opponent who is making the argument or when they themselves lack a good argument. Because *ad hominem* attacks are so emotionally charged, they often distract people's attention from the fact that the argument is based on a personal grudge or is in itself a poor argument.

The second fallacy is appeal to pity. People are often more persuaded by pity than by reason. Because of this, appeal to pity is one of the most powerful fallacies. This type of fallacy is often found in courtroom debates. For instance, let us say that Larry Jones is being accused of beating his children, but the prosecuting lawyer does not possess solid evidence demonstrating that Larry does indeed beat his children. That lawyer might try to stir up the emotions of the jury by saying something like this: "Ladies and gentlemen of the jury, you must convict Larry Jones of child abuse. Child abuse is a horrible crime. It scars children and ruins families." The lawyer might even show pictures of abused children and show statistics that indicate the terrible pain child abuse can cause. If the jury is not very critical, its members might get so emotional about the horrors of child abuse that they might convict Larry Jones, despite the lack of evidence, because they want to punish someone for this horrible crime. The fallacy of appeal to pity is committed when someone stirs up people's emotions to prove an argument without giving the audience solid evidence to prove the claim. While committing the fallacy of appeal to pity leads to poor arguments, it is sometimes appropriate to use some emotion in persuading people. For instance, if the lawyer in the example above had solid proof that Larry Jones had abused his children and then explained the tragic results of child abuse, stirring up the jury's emotions as a result, that would have been an appropriate use of emotion in an argument.

The last type of argument fallacy we will cover in this book is the straw man fallacy. When people commit straw man fallacies, they distort their opponent's argument to ridiculous proportions so it is easier to knock it down. For example, let's say that a child asks his parents if he can stay the night at the house of a new friend he has met at his school. Because the parents do not know this new friend or his parents, they respond, "Not this weekend. We need to get to know him and his parents before you spend the night." Infuriated, the child responds, "You don't want me to have any friends. You just want to lock me up in this house and turn me into a hermit!" The child has distorted his parents' argument to ridiculous proportions and has committed the straw man fallacy.

You might already be able to imagine how you could commit all of these common fallacies with the curfew debate. You might argue, just as the child in the last paragraph, that your parents don't want you to have any friends and want to turn you into a hermit. Or, you might use the pity tactic: "I am going to be so lonely this weekend. All of my friends will be hanging out together and I will be home alone. People will stop hanging around with me because they'll think I don't want to be friends with them anymore." This is both an appeal to pity and a slippery slope argument. If these don't work, you might even resort to *ad hominem* attacks: "You're so mean! You're unfair! You are the most overprotective, paranoid parents on the planet! And you have no sense of fashion!"

You might be feeling a little uncomfortable at this point because these arguments sound pretty familiar. In fact, you may realize that you have been the king or queen of fallacious arguments. If that is the case, don't despair because now that you are acquainted with some of the most common fallacies, you can be sure to avoid them.

DEFINE

Identifying Fallacies: Review all of the fallacies you have learned and then define each of them in the space provided.

1. Equivocation ____________________

2. Amphiboly: ____________________

3. Hasty Generalization: ____________________

4. Clichéd Thinking: ____________________

5. Illegitimate Appeal to Authority: ____________________

6. Bandwagon: ____________________

7. False Analogy: ____________________

8. Appeal to Moderation: ____________________

9. Snob Appeal: ____________________

DEFINE

10. Slippery Slope: ______________________________

11. *Ad Hominem*: ______________________________

12. Appeal to Pity: ______________________________

13. Straw Man: ______________________________

14. False Cause: ______________________________

15. Vagueness: ______________________________

16. Ambiguity: ______________________________

17. Accent: ______________________________

18. Distinction Without Difference: ______________________________

WRITE

Analyzing Fallacies: In the blanks provided, write the fallacy that is being committed in each of the provided arguments.

1. Wearing uniforms violates the very principles found in the United States' Declaration of Independence! After all, the Declaration says, "We hold these truths to be self-evident: that all men are created equal; that they are endowed by their creator with unalienable rights; that among these are life, liberty, and the pursuit of happiness."[1] Wearing uniforms does not allow me to pursue happiness. In fact, when I wear them, I am pursuing nothing but despair! Therefore, uniforms are against the very principles of our founding fathers.

____

2. He must be guilty of the crime. After all, he's a card-carrying member of the socialist party.

____

3. I don't know why I should even listen to your ideas about curfew. You just want to keep me locked up in this house forever! That way I will never leave the house and make any friends. I'll be like one of those guys who is still living with his parents when he is forty, and then you will always be able to boss me around!

____

4. You believe that capital punishment is right; I believe that it is wrong. It must be that it's wrong sometimes and right sometimes because that's a compromise.

____

5. My opponent promises to lower taxes. He tells you that he has a plan to reform education in America. He states that he will reduce crime. But what he does not tell you is that he was once arrested for drug possession.

____

6. I have this terrible headache. It must have been all of the sugar I ate this morning. In fact, I know it is because one time last week, I ate a doughnut and then I got a terrible headache.

____

7. I would like to remind America of my successful presidency. When I was elected, our economy was in a slump, yet at the end of my first four years as president, our economy was back on its feet again.

____

8. I believe that UFOs exist. My English teacher is really cool, and she believes in them.

____

9. Bob has this weird electrical energy that flows around his body. He just came into the room, and the lights went out.

____

WRITE

10. School is stupid. All of my friends think so, too.

---

11. Buy my miracle floor wax! My dear mother, who just passed away last month, God bless her, never used any other floor wax.

---

12. I'm absolutely certain I was obeying the speed limit, officer. If you give me a ticket, it will cost me over $500, and after paying a fine like that, I won't be able to pay for college. I will have to drop out, and I will not be able to get a job. I will become a terrible burden on society.

---

13. Fall is in the air and the winter chill is just around the corner. Everyone is buying Harbor Bay fall coats, the smart solution for beating the chill. When will you get yours?

---

14. Carson Meyers is going on trial tomorrow for armed robbery. If convicted, he will be put in jail for twelve years. He is supporting an elderly mother and three young children. Can we really put the welfare of his sickly mother and innocent children at risk?

---

15. Feminists say they want women to have equal pay with men in all situations. How ridiculous! What they really want is to enslave all men and then take over the world.

---

16. Senator Jones is asking us to enact stricter gun control laws. Our country is based on the basic and inalienable right of freedom of expression. Our forefathers died for these rights. How can we even think of despising their noble sacrifice?

---

17. A student says to his teacher, "You can't give me a 'B' in your class! If you do, I will never be admitted into the college I want to attend, and my dreams for being a pediatrician will be destroyed! How can you destroy my hopes and dreams that way?"

---

18. I can't believe I'm even listening to you! You can't even match your socks!

Congratulations! You are now familiar with all of the common topics and many of the common fallacies associated with them. In addition, you have developed many arguments that will aid you in your uniform debate.

There are a few things that you need to remember as you apply to future arguments the information you have learned in this book. Remember that when you need to think of arguments for a particular topic, you don't have to create them out of thin air. The common topics present you with a type of formula you can use to aid you in the invention of arguments. One of the best habits you can form as you learn to develop strong arguments is asking yourself a lot of questions about a position you are trying to prove. The common topics and subtopics give you a starting point for such questions.

Hopefully you have learned by now that as you approach every argument, you must keep in mind that no matter how convinced you feel about a topic, you may be wrong and your opponent may be wrong. More often than not, both sides of an argument have a mixture of correct and faulty beliefs. Therefore, you must approach arguments with a desire for truth and deeper understanding, even if that requires you to revise your opinion. You must also treat your opponent with dignity and respect, even if you decide in the end that you are right on every point, and your opponent is wrong.

Lastly, remember that arguments, although they have a bad reputation, can be positive. An argument is simply a reasonable explanation of the premises that lead to a conclusion. If you learn how to present these reasons well, and you proceed with humility and honesty, you will be way ahead of the game.

ANSWER

1. Who invented the common topics, and what is their purpose? ______________________________

2. How would you define deductive logic? ______________________________

3. What is a fallacy? ______________________________

4. Who first discussed the four idols? Why is it important to remember these idols as you argue? _

5. List and explain the four idols. ______________________________

ANSWER

Use a separate piece of paper if needed.

6. Write as many of the common topics and subtopics as you can remember, providing a brief definition of each.

7. Explain who John Stuart Mill was.

8. Explain four of the five methods John Stuart Mill developed for determining causal connections.

9. List and define at least seven fallacies that were discussed in this book.

WRITE

Your Debate Speech: Throughout the course of this book, you have studied each of the common topics, their various subtopics, and related fallacies and have practiced developing arguments based on these things to support a thesis about school uniforms. Now, you will use the various arguments you have drafted to participate in a debate with your classmates about this issue.

The first step in preparing for this debate is to write an essay that you will use as your speech. Throughout the course of this book, you have developed arguments about uniforms in school using all of the common topics. You will want to use your best arguments to develop your speech. For this first debate, everyone on your team should have three strong paragraphs supporting the thesis statement, and, of course, these paragraphs should not repeat information that someone else on the team has already shared. These paragraphs may develop an argument from just one of the common topics, or they may contain a variety of proofs from several different common topics. Before you begin writing your arguments, meet with the people on your team to make sure that you are not repeating any arguments. It is possible that in order for everyone to have three separate arguments for their speech, your group may need to generate some new arguments using the common topics. Once you have an idea of the arguments you will use, you can begin writing your speech.

On a blank piece of paper, start with an introduction. A simple way to begin is to state the thesis statement you developed at the beginning of this book. It may look something like this: "Uniforms help to create a good learning environment in school," or, "Uniforms do not help to create a good learning environment in school," depending on whether you will be argument for or against school uniforms. Once you write this thesis statement, you can lead into your arguments by writing a statement like this: "There are many arguments that support this thesis." Now you are ready to state your arguments. Take the three arguments that, along with the rest of your team, you have determined are you strongest, and write three fully developed paragraphs—one for each argument.

Now that you have written the body of your speech, you should end it with a concluding sentence. A simple conclusion could be a rewording of the thesis statement, like this: "Therefore, schools should adopt uniforms because they help form a good learning environment," or, "Therefore, schools should not adopt uniforms because they do not help form a good learning environment." A good concluding sentence such as this helps wrap up your ideas and provide a sense of closure for your audience.

Now that you have organized your speech, you need to read a little bit more about how debates work. So, go to Appendix: Holding a Debate for information about debating, and then your teacher will tell you how this particular debate will be structured for you class.

DEBATE

You have reviewed the common topics, written your speech, and consulted the appendix to learn how a debate is organized. Now it's time for you to participate in an actual debate. Remember that you should always approach arguments and debates with an attitude of humility and self-awareness. One of the most important things you can realize before you debate is that you might be wrong, and your opponent might be right. Good luck and have fun!

One of the most exciting parts of learning how to argue is the opportunity to participate in debates. *World Book Encyclopedia* defines a debate as "a series of formal spoken arguments for and against a definite proposition."[1] ("Proposition" is another word for a thesis statement.)

A formal debate is a debate that follows a set structure and has a judge who scores the arguments for both sides in order to determine who wins. A formal debate can occur between two people or two groups of people debating a certain thesis. There are several different formats that such a debate can follow, but most debate formats include time for both sides to present their arguments, as well as a rebuttal time in which both sides critique the opposing argument.

Although there are many different debate formats, most formats contain some similar elements. First of all, a debate is centered on a proposition or a thesis statement. This is a statement of opinion that can be proven true or false and which is usually worded positively. For example, a proposition for a debate on capital punishment would be worded this way: "Capital punishment is an effective crime deterrent." This is the positive way of making this statement, as opposed to the negative form, which would be: "Capital punishment is not an effective crime deterrent." To begin the debate, the affirmative side—the side that *supports* the proposition—presents its arguments first. After the affirmative side presents its arguments, the negative side, which opposes or disagrees with the proposition, presents its arguments. Sometimes, after the negative side has presented, both sides will present another set of arguments. The portion of the debate during which the arguments are presented is called the "constructive speech" segment. It is important to note that during this segment, the teams should refrain from making any comments or replies while the other team is presenting its arguments. Each side will have time to reply later.

After both sides have presented their arguments, they each engage in the **rebuttal** segment. In this segment, the team that opposes the thesis or proposition (the negative side), has the opportunity to present its rebuttals first. When you **rebut**, you critique your opponent's arguments. It may make you nervous to think that you will be required to critique your opposition's argument, but don't worry. The good news is that your study of the common topics has given you excellent skills for doing this, and, to some degree, you have already practiced this skill as you have determined the thesis of arguments, noted fallacies, and determined which argument from a group of several arguments is the strongest.

When you critique your opponent's argument, there are several main tactics that you can take:

1. You can show that your opponent is factually in error or that his information is incomplete.
2. You can show that your opponent's reasoning is weak or fallacious.
3. You can show that while your opponent has stated some truth in his case, your conclusions about the facts are stronger and fit the facts more completely.

Although being effective in rebuttals does require you to do some thinking on your feet, there are a number of ways in which you can prepare ahead of time. First of all, before the debate even begins, you should consider the key arguments that your opponent will likely bring against you. Of course, the best way for you to figure out those arguments is by using the common topics, just as you did as you developed your thesis statement. Don't worry, you don't have to write another complete essay or speech in order to determine those arguments. You just need to use the topics to brainstorm what the other side might say. Furthermore, during the debate, it will greatly help you if you take notes when the other side is presenting its speech. That way, you will be able to remember the key arguments and possible flaws of your opponent's arguments when it comes time for your rebuttal. Usually when a team rebuts, each person on the team speaks briefly about one or two argument flaws they detected in their opponent's argument. One person should not dominate the entire rebuttal time if other people on the team have something to say.

Another common format of debate is the cross-examination debate. While this debate format is very similar to the regular debate format, it differs in that after each group presents its main arguments, the other team is given time to cross-examine the arguments presented. This means that the other team gets to ask the opposing team questions about its arguments. When cross-examining the other team, you should ask questions about the other team's sources, their line of reasoning, and about unfounded assumptions that the team might be making. Most of the questions asked during the cross-examination time should be more in-depth than basic "yes" or "no" questions. It is important to realize that this cross-examination time is not a rebuttal. The team that is cross-examining the other side should not argue or make statements of opinion about the other team's arguments. It is purely a time for asking questions that may later help in disproving the opposition's arguments. Once both teams have presented their arguments and cross-examined the other team, both sides will have a chance for rebuttal.

Below is a list of the components of the two debate formats you have just examined.

Regular Debate Format

Constructive Speeches (10 minutes each)

1. First affirmative
2. First negative
3. Second affirmative
4. Second negative

Rebuttal Speeches (5 minutes each)

1. First negative
2. First affirmative
3. Second negative
4. Second affirmative

Cross-Examination Debate Format

Constructive Speeches (8 minutes each) and Cross-Examination (3 minutes each)

1. First affirmative
2. Cross-examination by negative
3. First negative
4. Cross-examination by affirmative
5. Second affirmative
6. Cross-examination by negative
7. Second negative
8. Cross-examination by affirmative

Rebuttal Speeches (4 minutes each)

1. First negative
2. First affirmative
3. Second negative
4. Second affirmative[2]

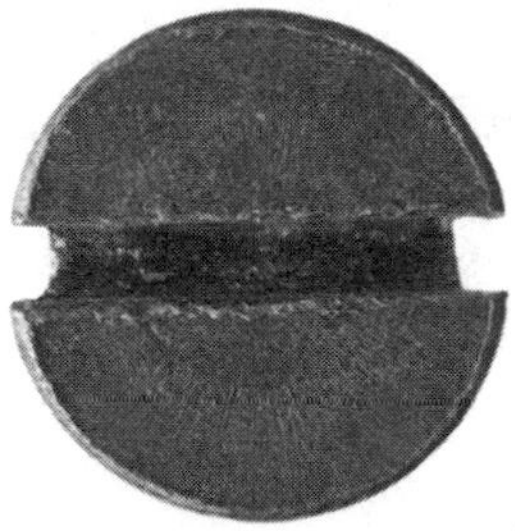

You should note that your teacher may change the time and format of the debate depending on your particular class' needs. For example, a class that is just learning to debate and only has a forty-five- or fifty-minute class period may only allow one opportunity for each side to present its argument, and this time may only last twelve or thirteen minutes. That time would be followed by time for a short rebuttal by each team. Your teacher can adjust the times and the order of the debate in order to fit your class' particular needs.

In order to prepare for a debate, there are several things you should do. First of all, you should summarize your speech into outline form. This outline will contain your main points, as well as any hard-to-remember facts, quotes, or statistics. Once you have composed this outline, you should practice your speech several times so that you are able to present your speech using your outline, rather than reading it word-for-word. You can accomplish this by practicing until you become familiar with the flow of your main points and the main ideas supporting each point. It is wise to practice your speech in front of the mirror and in front of others. When you practice both ways, it gives you a clearer picture of how you will sound to your audience. Realize that you do not need to say your speech exactly as it is written. You only need to be able to present the same general train of thought in your speech. In other words, the words you use when you present your speech may not be identical to what you wrote, but the ideas will be.

As you practice your speech, there are several things about your presentation that you will want to polish and perfect as much as possible. First of all, make sure you are standing up straight with both feet on the ground. Decide what kind of hand position will be most comfortable for you. Two of the best options are to keep your arms by your sides or, if a podium is available, to rest your hands on the top of the podium. You may also choose to keep them clasped behind your back. Avoid swaying, balancing on one foot, slouching or doing odd, repetitive gestures such as flipping your hair over your shoulder while you are speaking. It may sound funny, but people who are new to debates and speeches often unconsciously do these types of things things, as well as other distracting gestures. That is why it is good to practice in front of a mirror—you will be more likely to notice these things and make sure you don't do them during your presentation.

Next, work on making consistent and firm eye contact with your audience. As you become more familiar with your speech, you will be able to look at your audience most of the time, looking down at your outline only when necessary. Rehearsing in front of a mirror and with an audience is especially helpful for practicing eye contact. If you are nervous about giving speeches, practicing in the mirror first will help you get used to presenting a speech to someone, but it will be less intimidating because usually people are not scared of themselves! After you are a little more comfortable, you can practice your speech for your friends or family.

In addition to making eye contact, you want to pay attention to the volume of your voice, as well as the speed at which you speak and the clarity with which you enunciate your words. Be aware that in everyday life, people tend to speak quickly and softly, and they tend to slur their words together.

This is because usually, when we are talking to someone during the day, we are standing close enough to that person that she can understand what we are saying, even if we are not trying very hard to be clear. Unfortunately, this causes us to form some very bad speaking habits. Speaking on a stage, and to an audience, is very different from having a conversation with someone else. Being "on stage" changes the dynamics of speech in such a way that enunciating your words, speaking clearly, and adding appropriate pausing becomes essential. You do not want to deliver a whole speech only to have your audience wondering what you said after your first sentence. In order to make your speech clear, you should develop a "stage voice," that is, you should practice speaking slowly, clearly, and loudly enough to be heard at a fair distance. As you work on developing your stage voice it may feel like you are being overly dramatic, but it will help to ensure that your audience will understand you. You need to work on articulating every consonant clearly, pausing after every comma and period, and speaking slowly enough that you clearly form every word and give your audience time to register your words and phrases.

Once again, if you practice your speech several times, you will be able to concentrate on a different element of speech each time, which will help you to sharpen these skills. If you practice in front of an audience, ask them to tell you, at the end of your speech, two or three things that you need to improve. Getting immediate feedback in this manner can also help you become aware of odd and distracting speech habits that you did not know you had. Sometimes this can be a little uncomfortable, but it is much better to figure these things out with your family and friends than while you are delivering a speech in a formal setting.

As you are preparing for your first debate, realize that almost everyone feels nervous about speaking in front of others. Practicing speeches a lot and participating in many debates and speech events will help you overcome this fear, because you will know what to expect, and you will learn how to recover when you lose your train of thought or get distracted. Now go put all of your hard work into practice, and have fun!

ENDNOTES

Chapter 1: Foundations

1. George A. Kennedy, "Classical Rhetoric." *Encyclopedia of Rhetoric* (2001), 98.
2. Edward P.J. Corbett and Robert J. Connors, *Classical Rhetoric for the Modern Student* (New York: Oxford University Press, 1999), 491.
3. W. Martin Bloomer, "Topics." *Encyclopedia of Rhetoric* (2001), 779.
4. Aaron Larsen and Joelle Hodge, *The Art of Argument: An Introduction to the Informal Fallacies* (Camp Hill, PA: Classical Academic Press, 2003-07), 14.
5. Corbett and Connors, *Classical Rhetoric*, 18.
6. Larsen and Hodge, *Art of Argument*, 21.

Chapter 2: The Four Idols

1. Bryan Magee, *The Story of Philosophy: A Concise Introduction to the World's Greatest Thinkers and Their Ideas* (New York: Dorling Kindserly, 2001), 74-75.
2. Ibid., 77.
3. Ibid.
4. Corbett and Connors, *Classical Rhetoric*, 91.
5. David A. Fraser and Tony Campolo, *Sociology Through the Eyes of Faith* (New York: Christian College Coalition, 1992), 3.
6. "Chocolate is Good for You" [online]. *Health*. August 1999 BBC News. 13 July 2007. Available from: <http://news.bbc.co.uk/1/hi/health/413099.stm>.
7. Fraser, *Sociology Through the Eyes of Faith*, 7.
8. Magee, *Story of Philosophy*, 77.
9. Fraser, *Sociology Through the Eyes of Faith*, 4.
10. Magee, *Story of Philosophy*, 77.
11. Ibid., 64-5.
12. Kenneth R. Manning, "Florence Nightingale," *World Book Encyclopedia* (Chicago: World Book, Inc., 1992), 424-5.

Chapter 3: Definitions

1. Lewis Copeland and Lawrence W. Lamm, ed., "What Is an American?" by Harold Ickes, *The World's Greatest Speeches* (Minneola, NY: Dover Publications, 1973), 567.
2. Ibid., "On Woman's Right to Suffrage," by Susan B. Anthony, 321.
3. Henry David Thoreau, "Walking," 1862 [online]. Bartelby.com: Great Books Online, 13 July 2007. Available from: <http://www.bartleby.com/28/15.html>.

Chapter 4: Fallacies of Definitions

1. Phillip Johnson, *Darwin on Trial* (Downers Grove, IL: InterVarsity Press, 1991), 15.
2. Ibid., 13.
3. Irving Copi, *Introduction to Logic*. 5th ed. (New York: Macmillan Publishing Co, 1978), 112.
4. "The Complete Listing of Church Bulletin Bloopers" [online]. 27 August 2007. Available from: http://www.angelfire.com/tx4/BulletinBloopers/.

Chapter 5: Subtopic: Examples

1. Francis Bacon, "Of Empire," compiled by Darri Donnelly in "The Essays of Francis Bacon" [online], 1997. 18 April 2008. Available from: <http://ourworld.compuserve.com/homepages/mike_donnelly/lotFOUR.htm#empire>.

Chapter 6: Subtopic: Statistics

1. Jack R. Fraenkel and Norman E. Wallen, *How to Design and Evaluate Research in Education*. 5th ed. (New York: McGraw-Hill, 2003), 98.
2. Jane M. Healey, PH.D., *Failure to Connect: How Computers Affect Our Children's Minds—for Better and Worse* (New York: Simon and Schuster, 1998), 61-63.
3. Ibid., 61, 63.
4. Vern Brimley, Jr., and Rulon R. Garfield, *Financing Education in a Climate of Change* (Boston: Pearson Education, 2005), 16-7.
5. Fraenkel and Wallen, *How to Design and Evaluate Research in Education*, 185-6.

Chapter 7: Subtopics: Authority, Proverbs, Testimonials, and Scripture

1. Alan Loy McGinnis, *The Friendship Factor* (Minneapolis: Ausburg Publishing House, 1979), 15.
2. Francis Bacon, "Of Revenge" [online]. *The Essays*, edited by William Uzgalis. Oregon State University, Great Voyages Library. 13 July 2007. Available from: <http://oregonstate.edu/instruct/phl302/texts/bacon/essays_contents.html>.
3. Daniel Goleman, Richard Boyatzis, and Annie McKee, *Primal Leadership: Learning to Lead with Emotional Intelligence* (Boston: Harvard Business School Press, 2004), 10.

Chapter 9: Review of Definitions and Testimony

1. Richard C. Brown and Herbert J. Bass, *One Flag, One Land* (Morristown, NJ: Silver Burdett and Ginn, 1987), 152.
2. John C. Traupman, Latin and English Dictionary (New York: Bantam Books, 1995), 235.
3. Daniel Defoe, *Merriam-Webster Dictionary of Quotations* (Springfield, MA: Merriam-Webster, Inc., 1992), 229.
4. H.L. Menken, *Merriam-Webster Dictionary of Quotations*, 230.
5. Martin Luther King, *Merriam-Webster Dictionary of Quotations*, 229.

Chapter 10: Subtopic: Analogy

1. Francis Bacon, “Of Unity in Religion” [online]. *The Essays*, edited by William Uzgalis. Oregon State University, Great Voyages Library. 13 July 2007. Available from: <http://oregonstate.edu/instruct/phl302/texts/bacon/essays_contents.html>.
2. Augustine, “On Christian Doctrine,” *Great Books of the Western World* by *Encyclopedia Britannica*. Edited by Robert Maynard Hutchins (Chicago, London and Toronto: Encyclopedia Britannica, 1952), 627.
3. Ibid., 625.

Chapter 11: Subtopic: Differences

1. Michel Eyquem de Montaigne, “Of Fear,” *The Essays, Great Books of the Western World* by *Encyclopedia Britannica*. Edited by Robert Maynard Hutchins (Chicago, London and Toronto: Encyclopedia Britannica, 1952), 26.
2. John Ruskin, *True and Beautiful* (New York: Wiley and Halstead, 1858), 237.

Chapter 12: Subtopic: Degree

1. Corbett and Connors, *Classical Rhetoric*, 97-9.
2. Ibid.
3. Ibid.
4. Ibid.
5. Ibid.
6. Ibid.
7. Ibid., 99.
8. M.H. Abrams, ed. *Norton Anthology: English Literature*, “Death Be Not Proud” by John Donne (New York: W.W. Norton and Company, 1962), 1116.

Chapter 14: Review of Comparison

1. Brian MacArthur, ed. *The Penguin Book of Historic Speeches*, “I Have a Dream” by Martin Luther King, Jr. (London: Penguin Books, 1996), p. 488.

Chapter 15: Subtopic: Cause and Effect

1. G. David Roodman, "Blood." *World Book Encyclopedia* (Chicago: World Book, Inc., 1992), 26.
2. "Mill, John Stuart," *World Book Encyclopedia* (Chicago: World Book, Inc., 1992), 552.
3. Patrick J. Hurley, *A Concise Introduction to Logic* 7th ed. (Belmont, CA: Wadsworth Thomson Learning, 2000), 507-22.
4. Ibid., 507-8.
5. Ibid., 509.
6. Ibid., 511-12.
7. Brimley and Garfield, *Financing Education*, 26.
8. "Regular Naps Good for Your Heart" [online]. *Health*. February 2007. Digital Journal: Open Source Media. 13 July 2007. Available from: <http://www.digitaljournal.com/article/113290/Regular_naps_good_for_your_heart>.
9. Hurley, *Concise Introduction to Logic*, 505-6.
10. Lewis Copeland and Lawrence W. Lamm, ed. "Conciliation with America," by Edmund Burke, *The World's Greatest Speeches* (Minneola, NY: Dover Publications, 1973), 157.
11. Thomas Aquinas, "Treatise on God, First Part," *Great Books of the Western World*, Robert Maynard Hutchins, ed., (Chicago, London and Toronto: Encyclopedia Britannica, 1952), 13.

Chapter 16: Subtopic: Antecedent and Consequence

1. Aquinas, 12-13.
2. Montaigne, "That to Study Philosophy Is to Learn to Die," 28.
3. Ibid., "That the Profit of One Man Is the Damage of Another," 42.
4. Ibid., "Of Ancient Customs," 143.
5. Ibid., "Of Prayers," 152.

Chapter 17: Subtopics: Contraries and Contradictories

1. Aquinas, "Whether God Is Contained in a Genus?" 17.
2. Ibid., "Whether God Is Perfect?" 20.
3. Thomas Paine, "Common Sense" [online], Archiving Early America, 1996-2007. 27-09-07. Available from: <http://www.earlyamerica.com/earlyamerica/milestones/commonsense/intro2.html>.

Chapter 19: Review of Relationship

1. *Webster's Ninth New Collegiate Dictionary*, s.v. "Laugh" (Springfield, MA: Merriam-Webster, 1989).

Chapter 20: Subtopic: Possible and Impossible

1. Corbett and Connors, *Classical Rhetoric*, 108-9.
2. Ibid.
3. Ibid.
4. Ibid.
5. Ibid.
6. Copeland and Lamm, "Death of Socrates," 9.
7. Ibid., "Caitline to the Conspirators," 49-50.
8. Ibid., "God's Love to Fallen Man," by John Wesley, 154.
9. Aquinas, "An Argument for the Existence of God from Beginning and End," 13.
10. Ruskin, 296.

Chapter 21: Subtopic: Past and Future Fact

1. Eric Sevareid, "John F. Kennedy." *World Book Encyclopedia* (Chicago: World Book, Inc., 1992), 262.
2. Ibid., 110-1.
3. Ibid.
4. Ibid.
5. Ibid.
6. Copeland and Lamm, "Give Me Liberty or Give Me Death," by Patrick Henry, 233.
7. Augustine, "Whatever has been rightly said by the heathen, we must appropriate to our uses," 655.

Chapter 23: The Common Topics: A Cumulative Review

1. Richard A. Branyon, *Latin Phrases and Quotations* (New York: Hippocrene Books, 2001), 204.
2. *Webster's Ninth New Collegiate Dictionary*, s.v. "Friendly."
3. Ibid., s.v. "Friendliness."
4. Ibid., s.v. "Amicable," "Neighborly."
5. Anne E. Carr, "Mother Teresa," *World Book Encyclopedia*, 173
6. Ibid.
7. "Mother Teresa Quotes," *Brainy Quotes*, 02 December 2007. Available from: < http://www.brainyquote.com/quotes/authors/m/mother_teresa.html>.

Chapter 24: An Introduction to Other Common Fallacies

1. Brown, *One Flag, One Land*, 152.

Appendix: Holding a Debate

1. James M. Copeland, "Debate," *World Book Encyclopedia*, 64.
2. Ibid.

GLOSSARY *of Important Terms*

A

Accent: a fallacy committed when a word or part of a quotation is inappropriately emphasized or quoted out of context.

A Fortiori: from the Latin meaning "from the stronger," it is an argument from antecedent and consequence. It argues that a phenomenon will exist in a more probable situation because it exists in a less probable situation. The opposite may also be argued (e.g., the likelihood of the absence of a phenomenon in the more probable situation because of its absence in the less probable situation).

Ad Hominem: from the Latin phrase meaning "at the man," it is a fallacy committed when someone insults his opponent in an argument rather than disproving the opponent's argument.

Affirming the Consequence: a fallacy that occurs when a person affirms the consequence of a hypothetical statement without considering or allowing for additional factors, such as the following: If it is snowing outside, school is canceled. The first part of the statement is the antecedent. The second part is the consequence. If you affirm the consequence, you reason like this: If it is snowing outside, school is canceled. School is canceled; therefore, it must be snowing. This is a fallacy because other factors besides snow could lead to school being canceled. See also **antecedent**, **consequence**, and **denying the antecedents**.

Ambiguity or Ambiguous: a term used to describe a word or phrase that can have two or more meanings.

Amphiboly: a fallacy of definition that occurs when someone uses a vague, ambiguous phrase in two different ways within the same argument.

Analogy: an argument technique that draws a conclusion based on relevant similarities between two examples; a subtopic of comparison.

Anomalies: counterexamples that are exceptions or odd occurrences that don't fit a normal pattern. See also **counterexample**.

Antecedent and Consequence: an argument technique that draws a conclusion based on the natural implications of a situation or example; a subtopic of relationship.

Antonym: a word that has the opposite meaning of another word.

Appeal to Moderation: a fallacy that assumes that the correct answer is always a "middle ground" between two extremes.

Appeal to Pity: a fallacy committed when the speaker tries to convince an audience his argument is valid by making the audience feel sorry for him or for others.

Argument: providing examples or rational reasons for or against an idea or action with the intent to persuade.

Aristotle: a famous Greek philosopher who lived from 384-322 BC and developed the common topics. See also **common topics**.

Authority: an argument technique that uses the expertise of someone as evidence for a conclusion. "Authority" can also refer to a person who, through study and/or experience in a matter, has gained legitimate expertise; a subtopic of testimony.

B-C

Bacon, Francis: a philosopher who lived from 1561 to 1626 and who developed the scientific method and the idea of the four idols.

Bandwagon: a fallacy committed when a speaker argues that because everyone believes something or is doing something, we should believe or do it, too.

Bias: a predisposition in favor of or against someone or something.

Cause and Effect: an argument technique that draws a conclusion by demonstrating that one phenomenon caused the other; a subtopic of relationship.

Circumstance: a common topic that develops an argument by examining historical examples or what is likely to occur. See also **possible and impossible** and **past and future fact**.

Clichéd Thinking: a fallacy that occurs when the speaker attempts to apply a general rule, such as a proverb, as a formula that is applicable to every situation. This often results in ridiculous or trite reasoning.

Common Topics: a system Aristotle invented to help people discover all of the possible arguments for a topic. The five common topics are definition, testimony, comparison, relationship, and circumstance (see entries for each of these).

Comparison: a common topic that develops an argument by examining similarities, dissimilarities, and degree of similarity or dissimilarity. See also **analogy**, **difference**, and **degree**.

Conclusion: the part of an argument in which the speaker states what he or she believes.

Contradictories: a statement that uses the word "not" to oppose another statement by denying the other statement altogether.

Contraries: the opposite of a proposition that uses an antonym to express its opposite position.

Contraries and Contradictories: an argument technique that draws a conclusion from examining the contradictory or the contrary statement of a thesis; a subtopic of relationship. See also **contradictory** and **contrary**.

Counterexamples: examples that appear to disprove a thesis.

D

Deductive Logic: a method of determining the validity of a formal argument in which the conclusion must, necessarily, be true if the premises used to support it are true. Arguments are said to be "black" or "white" and cannot be gray. See also **formal logic**.

Definition: an explanation or illustration of a word. It is the first of Aristotle's common topics, and explores the meaning of a word in order to develop an argument. See also **antonyms**, **description**, **etymology**, **examples**, **genus**, **species**, and **synonyms**.

Degree: an argument technique that examines the relative worth of an example to determine the degree of its placement on scales of good and bad, practical and impractical, effective and ineffective, etc.; a subtopic of comparison.

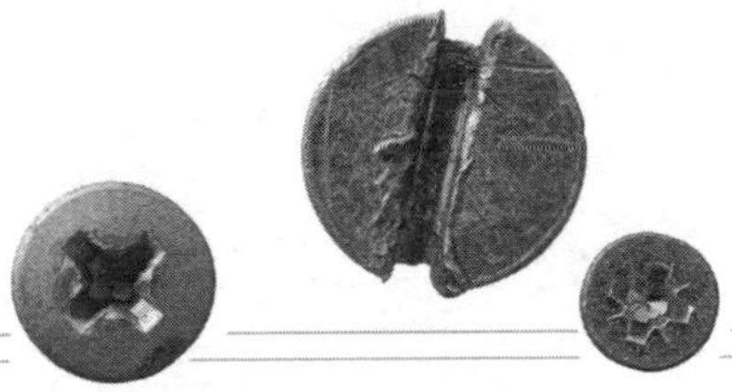

Denying the Antecedents: a fallacy related to affirming the consequence. In a hypothetical statement, such as, "If it is snowing outside, school will be canceled," a person commits the fallacy of denying the antecedent if they reason, "It is not snowing outside; therefore, school will not be canceled." This is a fallacy because, obviously, more factors than snow can lead to school being canceled. See also **affirming the consequence**.

Difference: an argument strategy that forms a conclusion from examining the dissimilarities between two examples; a subtopic of comparison.

Description: a definition technique used to explain a word in greater detail.

Distinction Without Difference: a fallacy that occurs when a speaker claims a difference between two examples when no difference actually exists.

E-F

Equivocation: a fallacy committed when a person uses alternative definitions of a word as though he was using one definition.

Example: a definition technique using an in-depth illustration to define a word.

Examples: a subtopic of testimony in which one looks to the past to figure out what to do. Also referred to as "precedent." See also **precedent**.

Etymology: the history and origin of a word.

Expert Opinion: see **authority**.

Fallacy: a commonly recognized type of bad argument; an error in reasoning.

False Analogy: a fallacy that occurs when an analogy fails because the two things being compared are too dissimilar. In other words, the two examples used to make the analogy are too dissimilar to be properly compared.

False Cause: a fallacy that occurs when a speaker uses a weak causal connection as the basis of an argument.

Formal Logic: one of the two branches in the study of logic centering on the "form" of an argument; it is reasoning in the abstract, focusing on deductive reasoning, where the validity of an argument is based solely on the structure (form) of the argument. See also **informal logic**.

Four Idols: an analogy developed by the scientist Francis Bacon in order to illustrate common errors in thinking. The four idols are the idols of the tribe, cave, marketplace, and theatre.

G-H

Genus: a large class that contains a wide variety of items sharing key similarities.

Hasty Generalization: a fallacy that makes a generalization about a class of things based on too few examples. See also **idols of the tribe**.

Hermeneutics: the art and science of interpreting the Bible.

I

Idols: objects of worship or extreme devotion.

Idols of the Cave: these idols represent our tendency to favor the views common to our particular class, ethnicity, or upbringing over any other views, which can hinder our ability to understand people who are very different from us. See also **idols of the marketplace**, **idols of the theatre**, and **idols of the tribe**.

Idols of the Marketplace: these idols represent our tendency to favor our interpretation of words over any other interpretation, which can lead to confusion in communication. See also **idols of the cave**, **idols of the theatre**, and **idols of the tribe**.

Idols of the Theatre: these idols represent our tendency to cherish the majority or established opinion over minority or novel opinion, which can inhibit our ability to relinquish flawed philosophies or paradigms. See also **idols of the cave**, **idols of the marketplace**, and **idols of the tribe**.

Idols of the Tribe: these idols represent the human tendency to engage in wishful thinking and hasty generalization. See also **hasty generalization**, **idols of the cave**, **idols of the marketplace**, **idols of the theatre**, and **wishful thinking**.

Illegitimate Appeal to Authority: a fallacy of testimony that is an illegitimate, or illogical, appeal to one individual expert. Usually this will involve an expert who is biased, not named, or whose competence is being transferred between unrelated fields.

Inductive Leap: a person's acceptance of an inductive argument, which results from premises that lead as closely to the conclusion as possible.

Inductive Logic: one of the two branches in the study of logic . It deals with ordinary language arguments that tend to start with evidence that can be observed and compiled and works toward generalizations that are reasonably accurate with more or less probability. Arguments are said to be either "strong" or "weak." See also **deductive logic**.

Informal Logic: deals with ordinary language arguments that tend to emphasize inductive rather than deductive reasoning. The structure or form of an argument is less the issue than the weight of the evidence, and the arguments are generally determined to be reasonably accurate with more or less probability. See also **formal logic**.

L-M

Legal Precedent: a legal decision that sets a pattern, or establishes a principle or rule, that a court adopts when deciding later cases that have similar issues or facts.

Logic: the art and science of reasoning.

Logician: one who practices logic.

Method of Agreement: a method developed by John Stuart Mill to test causal relationships; it examines phenomena sharing a common characteristic to determine the recurring factor causing the phenomena.

Method of Agreement and Difference: a method developed by John Stuart Mill to test causal relationships; combines the method of agreement and difference (see entries on individual methods).

Method of Concomitant Variance: a method developed by John Stuart Mill to test causal relationships; examines factors that appear to fluctuate simultaneously so that one increases as the other increases, or one decreases as the other decreases. One factor may also increase as the other decreases or vice versa. In these cases, one factor is usually the cause of the other.

Method of Difference: a method developed by John Stuart Mill to test causal relationships. A method that examines an example that lacks the characteristic of an observed example to determine which possible causal factor is absent in the example lacking a certain characteristic.

Method of Residues: a method developed by John Stuart Mill to test causal relationships; hypothesizes several possible causal factors for a phenomenon and then gradually eliminates all unlikely causal factors to determine the most likely causal factor.

N-P

Necessary Cause: a cause that must be present in order to produce a certain effect.

Operational Definitions: see **procedural definitions**.

Paradigm: a model that helps people understand complex phenomena.

Past and Future Fact: an argument technique that examines what has occurred in the past in order to draw conclusions about the present; a subtopic of circumstance.

Possible and Impossible: an argument technique that forms a conclusion by examining what is likely or unlikely to occur; a subtopic of circumstance.

Post Hoc Ergo Propter Hoc: the Latin name for the false cause fallacy. See also **false cause**.

Precedent: often referred to as the subtopic of examples, it is a subtopic of testimony in which one looks to the past to figure out what to do. See also **example**.

Prejudice: a positive or negative opinion formed before evidence has been carefully examined; often based on a hasty generalization. See also **hasty generalization**.

Premise: the evidence or proof supporting a conclusion.

Procedural Definitions: a definition technique that actually describes how something happens or occurs. Also known as "operational definitions."

Proverb: a wise saying that provides a general principle for living.

R

Random Sample: a sample in which all possible participants or examples in the study have an equal chance of being selected for observation.

Rebut: to contradict or oppose an argument, often by critiquing the various elements of the opposing argument.

Rebuttal: the act of rebutting; argument or proof that rebuts.

Relationship: a common topic that develops an argument by examining the connection or implication between examples. See also **cause and effect**, **antecedent and consequence**, and **contraries and contradictories**.

Rhetoric: the art of public speaking.

Rhetorician: a public speaker.

S

Sample: a group specially selected for a research study and which typically represents a picture of the general population.

Slippery Slope: a variation in the fallacy of false cause in which it is assumed that one step in a given direction will lead much further down that path without an argument being given for why one thing will inevitably lead to another.

Sophists: rhetoricians who focused more on the sound and style of a speech, rather than on the content. See also **rhetorician**.

Snob Appeal: a fallacy in which the speaker appeals to a sense of elitism or to those of "discriminating taste."

Species: a group of words having similar characteristics that distinguish them from other groups in the same genus. See also **genus**.

Statistics: the science of observing, organizing, and summarizing data into meaningful patterns; numbers that represent a large quantity of examples; a subtopic of testimony that represents an authority's summary of pertinent information. See also **authority**.

Straw Man Fallacy: a fallacy that occurs when someone distorts his opponent's argument to ridiculous extremes in order to make it easier to defeat or deny.

Sufficient Cause: a cause that may, but not necessarily, bring about a certain effect.

Syllogism: a deductive, formal argument consisting of two premises followed by a conclusion.

Synonym: a word that has the same or similar meaning as another word.

T-W

Testimonial: an average person's published experience (written or spoken) of a situation, product, or phenomenon; a subtopic of testimony.

Testimony: a common topic that develops arguments through examining the insight of famous or regular people. See also **authority**, **proverbs**, and **testimonial**.

Thesis Statement: a declarative statement of opinion that can be proven true or false.

Vagueness or Vague: a word describing a term that lacks precision because of overuse or because of its wide range of meaning.

Wishful Thinking: believing that something is true because you want it to be true rather than because the facts or evidence merit that belief.

GLOSSARY *of Important People*

A-L

Anthony, Susan B.: (1820-1906) An American civil rights activist who worked, specifically, for women's right to vote.

Aquinas, Thomas: (1225-1274) An Italian Catholic priest of the Dominican Order who is considered by many Catholics to be the greatest theologian and philosopher who ever lived. He is best known for his works *Summa Theologica* and *Summa Contra Gentiles.*

Aristotle: (384-322 BC) A Greek philosopher and student of Plato. He wrote on different subjects, such as rhetoric, logic, music, physics, metaphysics, poetry, ethics, biology, and zoology. He was one of the first people to systematize the study of logic and rhetoric.

Augustine: (354-430) A philosopher, theologian, and one of most important Church fathers. His most famous works are *On Christian Doctrine*, *Confessions*, and *The City of God.*

Bacon, Francis: (1561 to 1626) An English philosopher, essayist, and a proponent of the scientific revolution. He developed the scientific method. His theory of the idols attempts to describe beliefs that hinder human thinking.

Burke, Edmund: (1729-1797) An Irish statesman and philosopher known for his support of the American colonies against King George III and in the dispute that led to the American Revolution.

Copi, Irving: (1917-2002) An American logic professor in many key American universities. He is best known for his textbooks *Introduction to Logic* and *Informal Logic.*

Defoe, Daniel: (1661-1731) An English writer and journalist best known for works such as *Robinson Crusoe.*

Demosthenes: (384-322 BC) A Greek statesman and orator in ancient Athens.

Donne, John: (1572-1631) An English poet and preacher best known for his association with the metaphysical poets.

Kennedy, John F.: (1917-1963) The 35th President of the United States until his assassination in 1963.

Henry, Patrick: (1736-1799) An American statesman who played a prominent role in the American Revolution. He is best known for the speech "Give Me Liberty or Give Me Death."

Ickes, Harold: (1874-1952) An American political figure who helped to implement Franklin D. Roosevelt's "New Deal."

M-Z

MacArthur, Brian, ed.: *The Penguin Book of Historic Speeches*. London: Penguin Books, 1996.

Mill, John Stuart: (1806-1873) A British philosopher, political economist, and influential political thinker. In 1843, he wrote an influential logic book called *A System of Logic*.

Montaigne: (1533-1592) One of the most influential writers of the French Renaissance. He popularized the genre of essay.

Menken, H.L.: (1880-1956) An American journalist and satirist. An influential American writer as well as a critic of American life and culture.

Paine, Thomas: (1737-1809) A British writer and supporter of the American Revolution. He is best known for his work *Common Sense*.

Ruskin, John: (1819-1900) A British art and social critic whose essays on art and architecture were very influential in Victorian and Edwardian England.

Shakespeare, William: (1564-1616) An English poet and playwright. He is known as one of the greatest writer in the English language.

Smith, Will: (1968—) An American actor and musician known for recent movies, such as *I, Robot*, *The Pursuit of Happyness*, and *I Am Legend*.

Socrates: (470-399 BC) An ancient Greek philosopher known for laying the foundation of Western philosophy.

Thoreau, Henry David: (1817-1862) An American author, naturalist, and transcendentalist known for works such as *Walden* and *Civil Disobedience*.

Twain, Mark: (1835-1910) An American humorist and writer known for works such as *The Adventures of Huckleberry Finn*.

Wesley, John: (1703-1791) A British minister and Christian theologian. One of the greatest leaders of the Methodist movement.

BIBLIOGRAPHY

Abrams, M.H., ed. *Norton Anthology: English Literature.* New York: W.W. Norton and Company, 1962.

Aquinas, Thomas. "Treatise on God, First Part." *Great Books of the Western World.* Edited by Robert Maynard Hutchins. Chicago, London and Toronto: Encyclopedia Britannica, 1952.

Bacon, Francis. *The Essays.* Edited by William Uzgalis for Great Voyages Library. Oregon State University. 13 July 2007. Available from: <http://oregonstate.edu/instruct/phl302/texts/bacon/essays_contents.html>.

Bacon, Francis. "Of Empire." Compiled by Darri Donnelly in "The Essays of Francis Bacon" [online], 1997. 18 April 2008. Available from: <http://ourworld.compuserve.com/homepages/mike_donnelly/lotFOUR.htm#empire>.

Brimley, Vern Jr. and Rulon R. Garfield. *Financing Education in a Climate of Change.* Boston: Pearson Education, 2005.

Bloomer, W. Martin. "Topics." *Encyclopedia of Rhetoric.* Edited by Thomas O. Sloan. Oxford and New York: Oxford University Press, 2001.

Branyon, Richard A. *Latin Phrases and Quotations.* New York: Hippocrene Books, 2001.

Brown, Richard C. and Herbert J. Bass. *One Flag, One Land.* Morristown, NJ: Silver Burdett and Ginn, 1987.

"Chocolate is Good for You" [online]. *Health.* August 1999 BBC News. 13 July 2007. Available from: <http://news.bbc.co.uk/1/hi/health/413099.stm>.

Copeland, Lewis and Lawrence W. Lamm, ed. *The World's Greatest Speeches.* Minneola, NY: Dover Publications, 1973.

Copi, Irving. *Introduction to Logic.* 5th ed. New York: Macmillan Publishing Co, 1978.

Corbett, Edward P.J. and Robert J. Connors. *Classical Rhetoric for the Modern Student.* New York: Oxford University Press, 1999.

Fraenkel, Jack R. and Norman E. Wallen. *How to Design and Evaluate Research in Education.* 5th ed. New York: McGraw-Hill, 2003.

Fraser, David A. and Tony Campolo. *Sociology Through the Eyes of Faith.* New York: Christian College Coalition, 1992.

Goleman, Daniel, Richard Boyatzis, and Annie McKee. *Primal Leadership: Learning to Lead with Emotional Intelligence.* Boston: Harvard Business School Press, 2004.

Healey, Jane. M., PH.D. *Failure to Connect: How Computers Affect Our Children's Minds—for Better and Worse.* New York: Simon and Schuster, 1998.

Hurley, Patrick J. *A Concise Introduction to Logic* 7th ed. Belmont, CA: Wadsworth Thomson Learning, 2000.

Hutchins, Robert Maynard, ed. *Great Books of the Western World.* Chicago, London and Toronto: Encyclopedia Britannica, 1952.

Johnson, Phillip. *Darwin on Trial.* Downers Grove, IL: InterVarsity Press, 1991.

Larsen, Aaron and Joelle Hodge. *The Art of Argument: An Introduction to the Informal Fallacies.* Camp Hill, PA: Classical Academic Press, 2003-2007.

MacArthur, Brian, ed. *The Penguin Book of Historic Speeches.* London: Penguin Books, 1996.

Magee, Bryan. *The Story of Philosophy: A Concise Introduction to the World's Greatest Thinkers and Their Ideas.* New York: Dorling Kindserly, 2001.

McGinnis, Alan Loy. *The Friendship Factor.* Minneapolis: Ausburg Publishing House, 1979.

Merriam-Webster *Dictionary of Quotations.* Springfield, MA: Merriam-Webster, Inc., 1992.

"Mother Teresa Quotes." *Brainy Quotes.* 02 December 2007. Available from: <http://www.brainyquote.com/quotes/authors/m/mother_teresa.html>.

Paine, Thomas. "Common Sense" [online], Archiving Early America, 1996-2007. 27-09-07. Available from: <http://www.earlyamerica.com/earlyamerica/milestones/commonsense/intro2.html>.

Peterson, Houghston, ed. *The World's Greatest Speeches.* Simon and Schuster. New York, New York. 1954.

Piper, John. *Desiring God: Meditations of a Christian Hedonist.* Sisters, OR: Multnomah Press, 1986.

"Regular Naps Good for Your Heart" [online]. *Health.* February 2007. Digital Journal: Open Source Media. 13 July 2007. Available from: <http://www.digitaljournal.com/article/113290/Regular_naps_good_for_your_heart>.

Ruskin, John. *True and Beautiful.* New York: Wiley and Halstead, 1858.

"Sincere" [online]. About.com. 13 July 2007. Available from: <http://ancienthistory.about.com/od/etymology/f/Sincere.htm>.

Thoreau, Henry David. "Walking, 1862" [online]. Bartelby.com: Great Books Online, 13 July 2007. Available from: <http://www.bartleby.com/28/15.html>.

Traupman, John C. *Latin and English Dictionary.* New York: Bantam Books, 1995.

Webster's Ninth New Collegiate Dictionary. Springfield, MA: Merriam-Webster, 1989.

World Book Encyclopedia. Chicago: World Book, Inc., 1992.

Notes

Notes

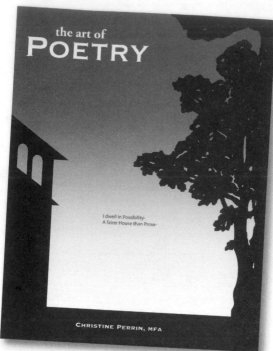

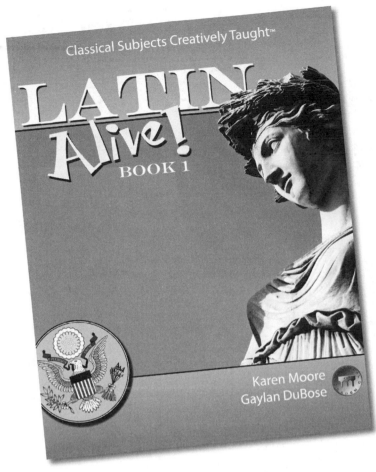

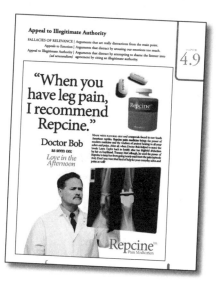